Advance praise for

Through Truth to Freedom: Reconciling a University's Past, Present, and Future

"To read Augsburg University's *Through Truth to Freedom: Reconciling a University's Past, Present, and Future* is both to admire and to be challenged by the integrity—the authentic wholeness—of its purpose. In this vision of 21st-century liberal education there is no separation of learning, citizenship, and neighborly love. Grounded in its Scandinavian Christian origins, its strikingly diverse neighborhood and student body, and its role as an anchor institution in Minneapolis/St. Paul, Augsburg exemplifies the truth that our universities best become national exemplars by embracing their particular place in the world: the land, the people, and diverse traditions that call us to be fully and faithfully human where we live now. By this standard, no other university can be Augsburg, but all of us can learn from its searching, honest, and reconciling commitments."

—William Craft, President Emeritus,
Concordia College

"This multi-disciplinary volume shows what is possible when we meet the past with critical yet ultimately loving eyes. The authors uncover a new narrative for Augsburg University that respects its history and its contemporary context. This book will be enjoyed by the Augsburg community but also by anyone with an interest in how institutions get better over time."

—Marjorie Hass, President,
Council of Independent Colleges (CIC)

"These essays illustrate Augsburg University's journey as a community-engaged institution, centering on the land and place that it calls home today. The institution's commitments to interfaith living, civic and community engagement, freedom of expression, and engaging across differences shine through ... and the story reinforces that Augsburg exemplifies the very best of what higher education can be and achieve when values don't just exist in mission statements and marketing materials but are lived out across every facet of the university community."

—Bobbie Laur, President,
Campus Compact

"The voices that are uplifted, the stories told, and the process of reflection serve both as an illustration of Augsburg's lived mission and a model for how other campuses can explore the intersection of truth and reconciliation as essential pillars of institutional renewal."

—Valerie Holton, Executive Director,
Coalition of Urban and Metropolitan Universities

Through Truth to Freedom

Through Truth to Freedom

· · · · · · · · · ·

Reconciling a University's Past, Present, and Future

BY PAUL C. PRIBBENOW
AND GREEN BOUZARD, EDS.

Myers Education Press

GORHAM, MAINE

Myers
Education
Press

Copyright © 2024 | Myers Education Press, LLC

Published by Myers Education Press, LLC
P.O. Box 424, Gorham, ME 04038

All rights reserved. No part of this book may be reprinted or reproduced in any form or by any electronic, mechanical, or other means, now known or hereafter invented, including photocopying, recording, and information storage and retrieval, without permission in writing from the publisher.

Myers Education Press is an academic publisher specializing in books, e-books, and digital content in the field of education. All of our books are subjected to a rigorous peer review process and produced in compliance with the standards of the Council on Library and Information Resources.

13-digit ISBN 978-1-9755-0695-7 (paperback)
13-digit ISBN 978-1-9755-0696-4 (library networkable e-edition)
13-digit ISBN 978-1-9755-0697-1 (consumer e-edition)

Printed in the United States of America.

All first editions printed on acid-free paper that meets the American National Standards Institute Z39-48 standard.

Books published by Myers Education Press may be purchased at special quantity discount rates for groups, workshops, training organizations, and classroom usage. Please call our customer service department at 1-800-232-0223 for details.

Cover design by Blaine Weber and Dan Ibara, members of Augsburg University's Design & Agency

Visit us on the web at **www.myersedpress.com** to browse our complete list of titles.

We dedicate this volume to the future generations of Auggies who will find in Augsburg's saga the truth and freedom to make a difference for the world.

Contents

Acknowledgments

This volume is the product of a 2 year conversation among 12 Augsburg University faculty, staff, students, and alumni. Together we interrogated Augsburg's historic saga and sought to make sense of its present and future. These were not always easy conversations, and we commend the participants for their candor, courage, and open minds as we both celebrated the good and lamented where the university had not lived up to its values and aspirations.

Each essay in this volume reflects the work of members of the saga group, some by solo authors, and others in collaboration. The volume is by no means comprehensive in its exploration of Augsburg's history. Combined, however, the essays reflect both the university's strong ties to the past as well as the complexity of its present as it has adapted to serve a diverse student body while also navigating the ever-changing landscape of higher education in the 21st century.

This project was generously funded with a grant from the Network for Vocation in Undergraduate Education (NetVUE), a program of the Council of Independent Colleges (CIC). Additional support was provided by the President's Strategic Fund, made possible by Mark and Margie Eustis and their family. The book cover was designed by Blaine Weber, a student in Augsburg's Graphic Design program, under the supervision of Professor Dan Ibarra.

We invite all who engage with this volume to join us in the critically important work of seeking truth and freedom by way of reconciliation.

Introduction

. . . .

To accept one's past—one's history—is not the same thing as drowning in it; it is learning how to use it. An invented past can never be used; it cracks and crumbles under the pressures of life like clay in a season of drought... The unprecedented price demanded—and at this embattled hour of the world's history—is the transcendence of the realities of color, of nations, and of altars.

—*The Fire Next Time*, James Baldwin

A t the conclusion of its sesquicentennial year in 2020, Augsburg University stood at the intersection of three pressing issues: the novel coronavirus that caused the COVID-19 pandemic; the ensuing economic disruption from the COVID-19 crisis; and the racial unrest occasioned by the murder of George Floyd a short distance from Augsburg's campus in Minneapolis. At this epicenter, the Augsburg community, which had experienced a radical transformation over the past decade in the profile of its student body to become one of the most diverse private universities in the country, looked to its future by interrogating the threads of its institutional saga—a saga shaped by its Norwegian ancestors, its Lutheran Christian foundations, its location as a dominant institution in a diverse immigrant neighborhood, and its decidedly Western liberal arts tradition.

What do we mean by an institutional saga? Throughout this volume, we use Burton Clark's definition of saga:

An organizational saga is a collective understanding of a unique accomplishment based on historical exploits of a formal organization, offering strong normative bonds within and outside the organization. Believers give loyalty to the organization and take pride and identity from it. A saga begins as strong purpose, introduced by a man (or small group) with a mission, and is fulfilled as it is embodied in organizational practices and the values of dominant organizational cadres, usually taking decades to develop. (Clark, 1972, p. 178)

In other words, a saga reflects the historic threads of an institution that create meaning for its present and future.

There is little doubt that Augsburg's historic threads define much of its current mission and identity.[1] The question is what in this saga can help us look forward to the sort of university our increasingly diverse students and community deserve for the next 150 years. How have the historical ways Augsburg thought about itself made it challenging to hear what our students and community need today? And, how do we decide what is good in our saga that should inform a path forward?

To answer these questions, a small group of faculty, students, staff, and alumni met monthly over 2 years to explore various aspects of Augsburg's institutional saga. Initially, members of the so-called "saga group" worked with the university archivist to identify an issue that seemed relevant to our present reality. For example, Augsburg was founded by Norwegian-American Lutheran Christians. What was found in that faith tradition that shaped the university's mission and identity? Where was this faith tradition still evident in the present daily life of the university? What in that faith tradition required us to wrestle with ways Augsburg had failed to live up to its highest aspirations, and how could we reconcile those failures?

After a year of exploring these historic threads, members of the saga group chose themes that they found most compelling and began to write essays that would appear in a published volume. Those essays were reviewed by the group and often led to further deliberations about whether and how Augsburg's saga was reflected in its present reality.

What became evident in these continuing deliberations is the central claim of this volume: that higher education institutions that seek to educate their students for freedom and liberation—the idea behind the liberal arts—must be prepared to embrace the truths they pursue and to lean into the reconciliation demanded by those truths. In other words, they must journey through truth to freedom, but only by way of reconciliation.

In 1969, during Augsburg's centennial year, the university framed its raison d'etre as the commitment to educate "From truth to freedom." For

Augsburg, this means providing an education for freedom grounded in claims of truth. Above all, these truth claims are grounded in the truth of the gospel of Jesus Christ—stated so powerfully in that founding scriptural motto from the first chapter of John's gospel, "And the Word became flesh and lived among us"—a truth that makes all things possible in our lives and work in the world. At the same time, truth for freedom is borne out in our commitment to a liberal arts education—to the belief in scientific knowledge, in social analysis, in artistic expression, and in cultural wisdom. And finally, the truth we rely upon we find in the lived experiences of our students and the communities from which they come—truths that reside in rituals, traditions, and practices that invite us into worlds rich in knowledge and wonder.

The questions we asked in our explorations delved deep into the heart of our faith tradition, our academic mission, and our commitment to social justice. Where is truth leading to freedom in the midst of the many challenges we face in the world? What truths for freedom are present in the struggles to keep each other healthy in the face of a novel coronavirus? Where is there truth for freedom in an economy that more and more creates remarkable inequities? What is the truth for freedom in centuries of systemic racism and oppression? Through appreciative and critical inquiry, the truths we discovered demanded that we reconcile with our past so that we might be freed for the work we are called to do as "informed citizens, thoughtful stewards, critical thinkers, and responsible leaders"—Augsburg's mission (n.d.)! We recognized over and again that the truth we sought often illuminated barriers to freedom in the present that required reconciliation.

We also found that this commitment to education for truth and freedom required us to embrace another familiar Augsburg motto: "Education for service," first coined by Augsburg's 6th President, Bernhard Christensen (Bouzard et al., 2023, p. 21). Throughout the essays in this volume, you will hear echoes of how reconciliation—the path to freedom—requires a servant perspective.

The result of this interrogation of Augsburg's saga is this monograph, comprising essays written by members of the Augsburg community—students, faculty, staff, and alumni—that lift up, explore, challenge, and appreciate how the threads of Augsburg's history set a path forward for the university. These essays address diverse aspects of Augsburg's saga, including its connection to its place, its faith tradition, its distinctive educational mission, its commitment to social justice for its students and community, and its consistent focus on welcoming those who are "first" to pave a path forward. At the same time, these essays offer a compelling example to other institutions about the important work of connecting past, present, and future—of seeking truth through freedom by way of reconciliation—work that is foundational to an institution's mission, identity, and future planning.

Though this volume focuses on Augsburg University's saga—and for that reason will be a most valuable resource for the diverse students, faculty, staff, alumni, and neighbors who comprise the Augsburg community—we believe these various essays also suggest both themes and methods for other communities that wish to wrestle with their institutional sagas. Through truth to freedom—by way of reconciliation— enables us to reshape the narrative of American higher education as we explore our commitments to particular places, faith traditions, academic missions, and public goods. We invite you to join us on this journey.

In addition to the essays here, we direct the reader to www.augsburg. edu/saga, a website that accompanies this book with links to resources that complement and extend the material in this volume, including archival materials, bibliographic recommendations, timelines, and maps.

Endnote

1.   The threads are evident in Augsburg's most recent strategic plan, "Augsburg150: The Sesquicentennial Strategic Plan," available at www.augsburg. edu/Augsburg150.

References

Augsburg University. (n.d.) *Mission Statement: The Augsburg Mission.* https://www. augsburg.edu/about/mission/

Bouzard, G., Clark, K., Pippert, T., & Pribbenow, P. (2023). *Radical roots: How one professor changed a university's legacy.* Myers Education Press.

Clark, B. (1972). The organizational saga in higher education. *Administrative Science Quarterly, 17*(2), 178–184.

Through Truth to Freedom:

By Way of Reconciliation

Paul C. Pribbenow

Common wisdom is that higher education in the United States is in trouble. The news is not good, full of dire warnings about student behavior, online learning, unhappy faculty and staff, budget challenges, and public skepticism about the value of a degree. In fact, the news and public opinion about higher education seems to foretell failure.

As a long-time university president, I am not naïve about the unprecedented challenges we face on our campuses and I give thanks for the tireless work of our students, faculty, and staff. I wonder if we might upend this failure narrative with a reminder of the unique role that higher education is called to play in moments just like this.

Augsburg University's motto is "Through truth to freedom," and I wonder whether and how we might recover its power for our academic and public missions, especially in a time when the relevance of higher education is being scrutinized. These words from Christian scripture were adopted as our motto in 1969 on the occasion of Augsburg's 100th anniversary at a moment when campuses and the country were reeling from similar forms of anxiety and unrest.

"Through truth to freedom" strikes me as a compelling response to this moment when we find ourselves living at the intersection of various pandemics. The novel coronavirus COVID-19 pandemic has disrupted all aspects of how we live and work and has pointedly illustrated the tension between public health and economic well-being. Following in the wake of the COVID-19 pandemic, an economic pandemic threatened our social fabric with massive unemployment and business closures worldwide. And, most recently, the racial inequities exacerbated by the senseless murder of George Floyd by Minneapolis police officers has created a third pandemic that threatens to tear our country apart. Surely this uncharted terrain presents unique challenges for all of us as citizens, trying to imagine how we will navigate to some as yet unknown future.

In a public presentation several years ago, Professor Mary Lowe from Augsburg's religion department offered a provocative challenge when she asked us what it might mean to educate our students for freedom. What a counter-cultural notion! Educated for freedom from ignorance, from oppression, from division, and from hatred and violence. Educated for freedom to make the world fairer, more just, and healthier; to be good neighbors; to take care of creation. Educated for freedom for the sake of the world, for the good of others, and for the promise of wonder and creativity.

But is this path through truth to freedom as linear as the motto seems to claim? Often, the search for truth uncovers separations and sins that demand reconciliation before there is freedom. This, in fact, may be the most important work for our colleges and universities: to educate for truth and freedom by way of reconciliation.

In his book, *Begin Again: James Baldwin's America and Its Urgent Lessons For Our Own*, Princeton professor Eddie S. Glaude, Jr. describes the lie that persists in the United States (Glaude, 2020). This foundational lie of white supremacy and its insidious implications is America's own original sin that must be confessed so that there might be reconciliation and finally, true freedom.

In our own Cedar-Riverside neighborhood in Minneapolis, our remarkably diverse Augsburg students and faculty engage every day with our immigrant neighbors—primarily Somali-Americans who are devout Muslims—and we witness their struggles with Islamophobia, with racism, and with poverty. It is only when we face and confess our own participation in the lies of white supremacy and other forms of oppression, that we find common ground, reconciliation, and the genuine opportunity to live as neighbors aspiring for freedom. This, I would argue, is the authentic work of democracy, an ethic of living "with" each other.

Through truth to freedom by way of reconciliation is, then, a fitting motto for all of American higher education in these times. The questions we will ask at Augsburg—questions at the heart of our academic mission and our commitment to social justice, and questions I believe all of higher education is poised to pursue—are about the truth to be found in the midst of these intersecting pandemics (and those that will inevitably follow), and the many challenges they pose to our mission-based work.

For example, what truths are there to be discovered as we anticipate keeping each other healthy during future public health crises? What truth is there to be found in an economy that more and more creates remarkable inequities? What truths do we encounter as we uncover the realities of centuries of systemic racism and oppression?

And in the ever-evolving, emerging, and transformative truths we will find, we must confront the sins and lies that we tell each other about knowledge, privilege, and justice. Only when we face the truths we find, confess our complicity in the sin and lies we tell, and humbly seek to be reconciled with each other and the creation, will we be freed for the important work we are called to do in the world.

That, it seems to me, is a much more compelling story of higher education in these times, and I can't wait to see all that we will do together to strengthen our university and our democracy.

References

Glaude, E., Jr. (2020). *Begin again: James Baldwin's America and its urgent lessons for our own time.* Crown Publishing Group.

What's in a Word:

. . . .

How We Tell Our Stories and Why it Matters

Katie Bishop

In 2013, Augsburg published its strategic plan, "Augsburg2019" (Augsburg University, 2013). The vision statement from the plan boldly stated that the next phase of Augsburg's work was to become a new kind of student-centered urban university—radically student-centered. This statement signaled a recognition that as Augsburg had made a commitment to serve the students in its neighborhood, particularly those who had been traditionally marginalized from higher education, it needed to build systems that provide meaningful access to the entirety of the college experience in ways that work for its students. Many of the systems of traditional higher education are founded on principles of exclusion, assuming that students enter college with sufficient money, time, and social capital to successfully access the rich experiences that form the heart of a college education. As many of the chapters in this book make clear, one thread of Augsburg's saga is its constant work to meet the needs of students, wherever they are at, to ensure meaningful access to a college degree.

A critical component of access to education is language. The words we use signal to our students whether or not they belong. However, the act of authoring a story is often to claim the privilege of gatekeeping. An author chooses which stories are told, whose voices are heard, and what language shapes the narrative. Unexamined biases and systemic exclusion are easily perpetuated and embedded in the ways stories are told.

Educational theorist Paolo Friere suggests that education is the act of thinking critically about one's place in the world and engaging with others to create new ways of knowing and action (Friere, 1970). As we consider the saga of Augsburg University, in order to live more fully into our desire to create belonging for all members of our community, we must interrogate the ways our own storytelling has used language in ways that exclude or marginalize the experiences of some and not others.

This essay serves two purposes. First, it explores the way past authors of Augsburg's history have told the story of Gerda Mortensen, Augsburg's first Dean of Women. I argue that the way her story has been told shows how language can marginalize the experiences of nondominant groups and individuals. It also acts, to use Stewart Van Cleve's beautiful words (see "Love Letters From the Past" in this volume), as a miniature love letter to the past, offering a new perspective on Gerda's story that repositions her as an innovative leader who laid the groundwork for much of what Augsburg does today.

In 1920 and 1921, Augsburg presented a survey to the Lutheran Free Church conference, its governing body, indicating that 81% of the Augsburg community believed Augsburg should admit women and become a coeducational institution. While the conference debated the issue, Augsburg was already accepting applications for admission from women. In 1922, the conference somewhat reluctantly voted to admit women, and five women enrolled at Augsburg for the first time. In 1923, Augsburg hired Gerda Mortensen as a faculty member in the history department and as the first Dean of Women. The new role was tasked with "guiding the integration of women into a student body with firmly entrenched masculine traditions" (Chrislock, 1969, p. 154). Unstated is the expectation that Mortensen would ensure the women were successful and didn't cause the governing conference to regret its decision.

Gerda Mortensen represents a number of "firsts" at Augsburg. She was the first female member of the history department, the first Dean of Women, and the first female senior administrator at the college. We have three accounts of her story at Augsburg. Her work at Augsburg is described in *From Fjord to Freeway* (Chrislock, 1969), *Hold Fast to What is Good* (Adamo, 2019), and in a series of interviews she gave to celebrate Augsburg's centenary. As we consider how authorship can be a form of gatekeeping by using language to frame information, comparing the way Gerda's story is told across these three sources is startling.

After one year in the position, Mortensen began taking Master's classes at Columbia University. In her own words, being new in the profession of student personnel management, she "needed to learn as much as [she] could in as short a time as possible" (Mortensen, 1969b, 1:24). She took courses in advising, institutional management to support the creation and management of residence halls, and vocational guidance. She would go on to become a local and national expert in the field of student affairs with a number of innovative programs that informed how the field developed. However, in past written histories of Augsburg, Mortensen's expertise and standing in the field are diminished and marginalized. For example, in *From Fjord to Freeway*, consider the language used to discuss the Dean of Men, John Melby, and Gerda Mortensen as Dean of Women.

> As Dean of Men, Melby largely ignored modern concepts of student personnel administration, but he possessed an intuitive understanding of youth that served him well . . . his enforcement of the more stringent rules was judicious. More important (sic), he cultivated a warm relationship with all students, most of whom responded favorably to his kindliness and the impression of sturdy manliness projected by his personality. (Chrislock, 1969, p. 154)

Compare this to the description of Mortensen's expertise:

> Her professional training, particularly the work she pursued in student personnel at Columbia University, where she earned the M.A. degree in 1928, put her in touch with modern counseling theory and practice, an interest she enthusiastically maintained throughout her career. (Chrislock, 1969, p. 155)

Finally, consider this description of their shared work as the deans of students crafting a new student handbook: "Melby and Miss Mortensen were moving toward more enlightened student personnel management during the 1930's, the former pragmatically, and the Dean of Women in accordance with modern theory" (Chrislock, 1969, p. 179).

In these passages, Mortensen's expertise is diminished when she is compared to her male colleague who is presented as having the same standing, leadership, and contribution despite their obvious differences in knowledge. While this undoubtedly mirrors the experiences Mortensen had during her career, needing to prove her value in a different way than her male colleagues, the language the author uses perpetuates that stereotype and diminishes her leadership, embedding a frame of reference about the value of Mortensen's work in the written story of Augsburg's history. This frame of reference for her leadership being less valuable because she was a woman is used more explicitly when discussing her work.

In the beginning, Mortensen's role was to successfully integrate women into the campus community. One could interpret that role as one of teaching women how to be part of a college campus without creating problems, a variation of teaching women to "know their place" even as they were granted admission to the college. As women were first accepted to the institution, there was pressure to ensure the female students were successful in every aspect of their college participation, in part to show that the conference had made the right decision in allowing their admission. That was part of the reason for creating the role of Dean of Women. To accomplish this aspect of her task, Mortensen "soon became convinced that [there needed to be] an effort to cultivate a more collegiate way of life on campus, a goal requiring modification of rural immigrant values with respect to dress, manners, and social graces, [which] had to accompany the integration process" (Chrislock, 1969, p. 154). In *From Fjord to Freeway*, rather than being described as a political imperative, this work is described as a project to "create social refinement." The author comments that "not all members of the Augsburg community agreed that social refinement was an appropriate educational goal, and most of Miss Mortensen's colleagues were unaccustomed to leadership by women faculty members" (Chrislock, 1969, p. 154). Here again, the author positions this work as rightly having its value questioned. There is no commentary that this project was necessary to accomplish the goals of her position, nor discussion of the skill it required to get the faculty to pass this educational program.

In *Hold Fast to What is Good*, the author treats this particular aspect of Mortensen's work in a remarkably similar manner. The author discusses the idea that Mortensen struggled as the first female administrator at Augsburg, particularly in pointing out that her speeches were not recorded in the same way as her male colleagues. Her thinking on the role of women in society is shared via a speech she gave on WRHM radio: "If young women worked hard, they could be unimpaired by the inhibitions of the past, undismayed by destructive criticism of the present and unafraid of the future" (Adamo, 2019, p. 58). The text goes on to comment, "In a time when strong women didn't always get the same opportunities as men, Mortensen's words would ring true for herself, as well as the female students who studied at Augsburg in the decades to come" (Adamo, 2019, p. 58). The author then describes the social refinement program and comments, "One wonders whether these were the most pressing issues women faced in the 1930s?" (Adamo, 2019, p. 58). This author names the framing more explicitly, calling into question the value of Mortensen's leadership and contribution to the college.

The discussion of Mortensen's contribution to Augsburg and the broader student affairs community in *Hold Fast to What is Good* ends with the following words:

> Yet her life also had a kind of feminist undercurrent. In spite of the extent to which Mortensen focused on training women to be gracious helpmates to men, she herself never married. She was dedicated to her work and was a living example of a successful woman, fulfilled by her professional life. She also raised two nieces and was the "adopted" mother to hundreds of young women who were her students. (Adamo, 2019, p. 59)

Mortensen's leadership at Augsburg is reduced to being first and foremost a woman, her leadership understood in the context of the value men placed on it, and ends with a framing of her positionality that understands her identity in the context of presumed motherhood, despite the fact that she never had children, and in her own interview, did not express any sentiment towards her students that could be considered mothering.

Gerda Mortensen worked at Augsburg for over 40 years. In that time, she successfully shepherded the integration of women into the institution, built and managed residence halls, and developed a residence life program. She was the first female administrator and first female member of the history department. She pioneered a program with volunteer nurses to provide healthcare to Augsburg students, an idea that fore-shadows Augsburg's deep commitments to community engagement in programs such as the Health Commons, which is described in the chapter later in this volume entitled, "Augsburg's Health Commons: Caring for Our Neighbors in a World of Extremes."

In Gerda's own words, "Augsburg was something which I always knew about, I don't know when I learned how to read. I don't know. When I first heard about Augsburg, it was just something that was a part of us. It was more than a school. It was a place. It was an institution. It was a feeling; it was a conviction" (Mortensen, 1969a, 1:36). Many of the people who work at Augsburg today resonate with these words, as deeply committed to its mission as Gerda Mortensen was.

We are fortunate to have an oral interview with Gerda. As I listen to her telling her own story, I feel deeply the subtle ways that she had to regularly fight for her seat at the table. The following story paints that struggle in vivid color: As a result of Mortensen's training at Columbia, she presented a plan to the faculty at Augsburg to create the first iteration of student affairs, focusing on all aspects of student personnel. The faculty voted to start the program and when it was presented to President Christensen, he said, "I hear you voted yourself out of a job yesterday. [Gerda asked] Do you intend to have women students anymore? [Christensen replied] Well yes, but if you have a student personnel program then you have to have a man at the head of this and then you won't need anyone else." (Mortensen, 1969b, 22:53) During the interview, Mortensen makes the following comment to this story: "Well, this showed how terribly little understanding there was of all the things that are involved in the student personnel program" (Mortensen, 1969b, 23:07). Mortensen shares this in a matter-of-fact way that speaks volumes about the constant challenges she faced and the grace with which she handled them.

Our words matter. They convey to the reader what to value and what to diminish. As Augsburg charts a path into its future as a diverse institution serving students who have traditionally been marginalized, it is critical that we conceptualize a use of language and authorship that is inclusive, rather than one that perpetuates biases. Perhaps the case of Gerda Mortensen provides an insight: when we allow individuals to speak for themselves, bringing their own language and authentic experiences into their education, we will have a more inclusive space that creates a sense of belonging for all members of our community.

References

Adamo, P. (2019). *Hold fast to what is good: A history of Augsburg University in ten objects.* Augsburg University.

Augsburg University. (2013). *Augsburg 2019.* https://www.augsburg.edu/augsburg2019/

Chrislock, C. (1969). *From fjord to freeway: 100 years Augsburg College.* Augsburg College.

Friere, P. (1970). *Pedagogy of the oppressed.* Continuum.

Mortensen, G. (1969a, July 29). *Oral History Interview with Gerda Mortensen (1 of 4)* [Audio recording]. Augsburg University Archives. Minneapolis, MN, United States. https://archives.augsburg.edu/islandora/object/AUGrepository%3AoralhistoriesAugsburgMemoriesGerdaMortensen1969

Mortensen, G. (1969b, July 30). *Oral History Interview with Gerda Mortensen (2 of 4)* [Audio recording]. Augsburg University Archives. Minneapolis, MN, United States. https://archives.augsburg.edu/islandora/object/AUGrepository%3AoralhistoriesAugsburgMemoriesGerdaMortensen1969

Love Letters From the Past:

. . . .

The Role of an Institution's Archives

Stewart Van Cleve

Thirty years after its move to Minneapolis, Augsburg Seminary cele-brated the start of the 20th century with a 3 day dedication ceremony for the newest building on campus. A book published in 1902 to commemorate the occasion offered a breathless tour of the state-of-the-art facility, noting new luxuries for faculty and staff that included hot running water and electric lights. Perched on a small hill at the corner of 8th Street and 21st Avenue South, the building's classical symmetry was resplendent in Kasota limestone, pressed brick, terra cotta, galvanized iron, and stained glass. Inside the new Main Building, a two-story central atrium with glass floors allowed light to shine from a skylight down to the first floor ("The New Building," 1901–2). That light did not reach the lowest level, where the gymnasium, the boiler room, the library, and restrooms with bathing facilities were located. The basement also included a small space next to a stairwell for "the nucleus of the Augsburg museum," where the seminary deposited a growing pile of items ("The New Building," 1901–2, p. 7).

There are few references to—and certainly no inventories of—what the museum held. An *Augsburg Echo* article published in 1940 claimed the collection had grown to include a tiger skin, a model ship, a deer head, a stuffed eagle, a spinning wheel, and a (hopefully disarmed) shell from the First World War that "only Superman could lift" (Krohn, 1940). It also included a collection of artifacts that were taken from Madagascar and India by Lutheran missionaries and placed in glass display cases ("Locals," 1914, p. 24). By then, the museum had moved into the attic of New Main to make room in the basement for something more important.

In the spring of 1929, Professor Andreas Helland met with three other men to create a new organization at Augsburg Seminary. Their "Archive Society" sought to gather books, periodicals, documents, and items for storage in the old museum space, which had been renovated to become "fire safe." "With sufficient means a great work can be done in augmenting and improving the collection," a 1930–31 Seminary Catalog noted, "especially in the way of buying books and binding of periodicals" (p. 26). Perhaps anticipating those "sufficient means" would take a while to accumulate, the catalog ended its announcement with a request for donations (Augsburg University, 1930-31, p. 26). The Archive Society collected academic records, business records, faculty publications, and Norwegian Lutheran works, and it had plans to display the "Mission Museum" in a more prominent location at a later date.

In a twist of fate guided by decades of unseen hands, the catalog that announced the formation of the Archive Society is now part of the collection it founded. It remained in New Main for almost long enough for the building to become "Old Main" before it moved to the Science Hall in 1949, then to the modern Sverdrup Library (now Sverdrup Hall) after that building opened in 1955 (Sverdrup Library, Archives, ca. 1955). Four decades later, it crossed 7th Street to Lindell Library, the latest library building, where it remains to this day (Hogan, 1998b).

The shepherds of Augsburg's archives carried a collection that grew as it moved across four buildings, weaving serendipitous and paradoxical histories that form a repository of gifts and challenges. As evidence of the truth itself, and despite archivists' best efforts, archival collections can be quite messy and difficult to understand. They should inspire us, trouble us, challenge us, and comfort us in equal measure. Navigating these many contradictions is certainly the work of writing an institutional history, but it is also key to learning, the very freedom that higher education provides.

Augsburg's archivists have rarely received credit for their dedication to preserving the institution's past. While Andreas Helland had the privilege of being the first to lead efforts to establish formal archives, a team handed the collection down from one generation to the next. By 1960, the responsibility fell to Agnes B. Tangjerd, the head librarian and a member of the faculty. She held two college degrees, taught courses in library science, and managed all aspects of library services for more than 1,200 people (Augsburg University, 1940–41, p. 7, 49; "Fall Enrollment Up," 1960, p. 4). Near the end of her career, Tangjerd became the College Archivist and in that role she helped researchers, including Carl Chrislock, author of 1969's *From Fjord to Freeway* (a seminal history of Augsburg), write their histories without ever writing her own (Evenson, 1968, p. 3).

At the end of the 20th century, a pair of Andersons moved the collection to Lindell Library. One, Dr. Kristin Anderson, has served on the faculty in the art and design department since 1983. She became the College Archivist in 1997, closing a 13 year gap after Ruth Futcher left the post due to a lack of funding. By then, Dr. Anderson had spent more than a decade teaching art and art history courses, coordinating exhibitions and workshops from visiting artists, and sharing her interdisciplinary expertise on art history, architectural history, Scandinavian studies, and women's studies. The other Anderson, Charles, had just retired as Augsburg's eighth president. He led efforts to dramatically improve campus through the 21st Century Fund campaign, culminating with the James G. Lindell Family Library in 1997. Rather than spend his days in well-earned relaxation with a good book, "Chuck" joined Dr. Anderson (who was also his daughter) and moved the archives from Sverdrup to their new home in Lindell's basement (Nelson & Wood, 2000, p. 24). In all, they hauled hundreds of records boxes, books, recordings, furniture, and works of art (Nelson & Wood, 2000, p. 24).[1] In an interview with *Augsburg Now* at the time of the move, Dr. Anderson shared her dream of an endowment for the archives and a dream to make the collection accessible using a computer.

Twenty-five years later, the endowment remains a work in progress, but we can read this story and enjoy links to digitized archival references thanks to the groundbreaking work of a librarian named Bill Wittenbreer. When he started working at Augsburg a few years after Lindell Library opened its doors, the concept of accessing archives online had only recently emerged. By 2013, online accessibility had become an obvious need, so Wittenbreer acquired equipment, hired student employees, and transformed brittle pages of history, one by one, into a searchable online database (Tetzlaff, 2017). Just 4 years later, when he retired, his team had scanned more than 30,000 pages, including all available issues of *The Echo*, Augsburg's student newspaper, since it was first published (in Norwegian) in 1898, as well as literary magazines, course catalogs, and alumni magazines.

Wittenbreer's team also scanned all 77 editions of the *Augsburgian*, the annual yearbook published from 1916 to 2010 (with a few budget-related interruptions). These essential books are substantive and stylistic snapshots of Augsburg's history, giving us alphabetized portrait galleries of students, faculty, staff, guests, and board members. Richly illustrated with photographs, the yearbooks include sections for student organizations, athletics, and notable events that took place each academic year (Augsburg University, n.d.). They are the first place to look when researching Augsburg's history during the 20th century and, thanks to Bill Wittenbreer's years of meticulous work scanning each page, the entire collection is available to anyone with internet access.

Important as they are, the yearbooks are not comprehensive historical records of Augsburg. They were created by dedicated student committees that made choices on what to cover and what to ignore, leaving behind noticeable gaps in the historical record. Notably, and along with other collections in the archives, the yearbooks reveal occasions when our historically white institution showed its ignorance. Records of parties, parades, skits, and certain yearbook photos show times when Augsburg's students were entirely too comfortable mocking people who were different from themselves. It may be uncomfortable, but we must take a closer look at this important aspect of our past.

In the 1948 edition of the *Augsburgian*, found among portraits and campus scenes that we might expect, the editors included a dozen cartoon images of Native American stereotypes that decorate the margins. These cartoons include "chiefs" brandishing sticks, smoking peace pipes, or imitating participation in a debate, as well as bare-chested "warriors" who play drums, struggle to ice skate, or react with surprise as arrows strike their rears (pp. 13, 70, 71, 77, 78, 84, 86, 88, 90, 91, 92). Not satisfied with limiting racism to that particular yearbook, Augsburg continued the following year with its Homecoming theme, "Redmen Behind in '49." This was a reference to St. Mary's football team, the Redmen, one of many teams that adopted a racist name or mascot until St. Mary's changed the team to the Cardinals in 1989 ("What's in a name," n.d.).

Though Auggies did not create that name, it gave them a platform to bring institutionalized racism into the open. A preserved and digitized film reel of the 1949 homecoming parade includes scenes of Native American effigies wrapped in blankets and placed in a canoe, as well as a white student in redface who waves a stereotypical *háu* to cheering spectators as the parade circled Murphy Square (Augsburg University Archives, 2019, 9:20). The idea might have been to roast the opposing team, but that homecoming parade dug us deeper into a legacy of historical cruelty, mocking Minnesota's Indigenous ancestors on land that was taken from them.

The park in the center of campus was again the site of racist mimicry during an outdoor costume party that was likely held on Halloween, and which is documented in another archived film reel. Scenes of the crowded festivities include a few frames showing one student in blackface as another milled about in a poncho and sombrero ("School activities at Augsburg," 1948–49, 8:20). Students donned blackface in at least two other documented instances: during a skit captured on film in 1949 and in a 1959 *Augsburgian* photo that shows two white students dressed as "African Royalty" during a skit performed for first years ("Winter Sports," 1949, 7:33; "Party for the Greens," 1959, p. 21). A particularly chilling instance of anti-Black racism can be found in the 1958 *Augsburgian*. One of the portraits includes a deeply disturbing mask of "Zeni Yerruc," a fictional student from "Naigrubsgua, Africa" that is at once surreal and upsetting to see firsthand (Augsburg University, 1957).[2] The comfort white people felt as they mocked BIPOC people as "others" continued into at least the 1960s when the annual campus carnival included a "Geisha House" that advertised backrubs (Augsburg University, 1966, p. 38). These are certainly not the only times that racist behavior surfaced here. They are notable simply because they were captured on film.

It may tempt some to excuse this behavior as being from "a different time," or that the people who created those drawings, effigies, and costumes did not intend to cause harm. It is important to understand the historical context and the creators' intent as we find items in the archives, but it is equally important to consider the different perspectives of those who witnessed those events as they were memorialized, even if there is no available record of how all witnesses felt. We should, for example, think of students and faculty of color who were becoming "firsts" at Augsburg in the late 1940s and 1950s, when this behavior was taking place. How did Augsburg's first Black students, including Jim Nichols and Richard Green, respond to seeing depictions of "African savages" in their yearbooks? How did they feel, knowing they were surrounded by white people who either exhibited overt racist behavior or condoned it in their silence?

These questions are some of many that we, unfortunately, have limited capacity to answer. The archives are stuffed with more than 150 years of history, but they are still limited by what historical records found their way into the collection. We do not have a great deal of information, for example, on one of the earliest student organizations that highlighted the leadership of Augsburg's students of color. Formed as the "Cosmopolitan Club" in 1954, it organized social activities for international students (at the time referred to as "foreign" students) who generously offered to share their cultures with the Augsburg community at a time when it was still an overwhelmingly Norwegian-Lutheran institution ("Cosmopolitan Club," 1954). Aside from a handful of articles in *The Echo* and photographs in the *Augsburgian*, we have little information on the club, its members, or their important work as they built foundations for the student diversity that Augsburg is known for today.

Another absence in the archives is a missing collection of film reels that I have struggled to find for several years. In the late 1950s, as many American households were enjoying their first black-and-white television sets, nonprofit television stations began cropping up in several major U.S. cities. These "educational television" broadcasters brought knowledge and culture that was once limited to libraries, classrooms, and radios to the comfort of viewers' living rooms. In 1955, Twin Cities Area Educational Television began to operate on Channel 2, and, two years later, a group of Minnesota private colleges and universities joined forces to offer the *Minnesota Private College Hour* on the new network (Alburn, 1955).

It was a revolution in higher education. Starting with an hour-long evening block every weekday from 8 pm to 9 pm, the *Private College Hour* offered credit-bearing instruction delivered by faculty from 14 participating institutions via live telecast ("Area colleges," 1957, p. 4). Augsburg contributed to the immediate popularity of the series, which piqued enough interest to lead a newspaper editor in Austin, Minnesota to complain that the signal did not reach them 100 miles away ("Thoughts at random," 1958, p. 6). Two women of color deserve recognition for Augsburg's participation in the early years of remote learning: Dr. Irene Khin Khin Jensen and Professor Mimi Baez Kingsley.

Born in Burma (Myanmar) in 1925, Dr. Jensen began her college education at Rangoon University, only to be interrupted by the Japanese invasion during the Second World War. After spending years as a refugee in southern China, she returned to her studies, completed her bachelor's with honors, and then came to the United States as a Fulbright Scholar in 1950 (Jensen Kantar, 2018). After meeting her husband, Augsburg alumnus Vernon Jensen '47, and passing her final doctoral examination (delayed by only 3 weeks after she gave birth to her first child), Dr. Jensen began teaching history at Augsburg in 1956 (Hunter, 1956, p. 14). With a keen interest in educating the Twin Cities community about Asian history and culture, and in the context of the United States' deepening involvement in the Vietnam War, Dr. Jensen's program on the *Minnesota Private College Hour*, "Southeast Asia Today," was well received. It aired for five episodes in 1959–1960 and made Dr. Jensen one of the first AAPI women— if not the first—to present via local television in Minnesota ("KTCA to start new series," 1959, p. 13a).

A colleague of Dr. Jensen, Professor Mimi Baez Kinglsey, had a similarly impressive resume. Born in Pachuca, Mexico, her education included Maryville College, the University of Mexico, the University of Minnesota, and Columbia University. She began Spanish instruction at Augsburg when she started teaching in 1947 and earned respect for the difficult work of "making the Spanish language and culture significant to a predominantly Scandinavian community" ("Augsburg mourns loss," 1969, p. 1; "'Latin from Manhattan'," 1968, p. 1). Professor Kingsley was also an early advocate of study abroad for Augsburg students and was a longtime faculty advisor for the Student Project for Amity Among Nations (SPAN) (Storlie, 1962, p. 3). She joined the *Minnesota Private College Hour* in 1958, teaching a twice-weekly course called "Spanish for Conversation" ("Town toppers," 1958, p. 23). Her course was so popular that, according to Carl Chrislock, it "added impetus" for Augsburg to add another year to its language requirement for undergraduates. It also helped inspire the administration to restore language majors to the curriculum (Chrislock, 1969, p. 216).

I wish I could share digitized versions of these women's telecast lectures. Doing so would give them each space to speak to us across time and with their own words. Sometimes, as in the case of Gerda Mortensen, the first Dean of Women at Augsburg, we are fortunate that the archives include oral histories (see the chapter in this volume "What's in a Word: How We Tell Our Stories and Why it Matters" for more about Gerda Mortensen and the importance of her presence in the archives, as opposed to the account of official institutional historians). To date, I am unable to find the same type of resource for Dr. Jensen or Professor Kingsley. With threadbare budgets and limited space in their early years, local television studios did not save copies of kinescope films used in telecasts. Of thousands of hours of programming aired on the *Minnesota Private College Hour*, a mere handful of films have been preserved in archives around the state. The rest are missing and presumed lost. None, to date, are in Augsburg's archives.

Perhaps one day, as someone is clearing out an office or preparing for a long-overdue renovation in Memorial or Old Main, the door to a forgotten closet will reveal a pile of rusting film canisters with faded blue KTCA logos. It may seem like a stretch, but that is exactly what happened when the archives received a collection of nearly 500 aging reel-to-reel audiotapes in 2016. They were pulled from a utility closet in the basement of Sverdrup Hall and dated back to when the space was the audiovisual collection of Sverdrup Library. Among the invaluable knowledge contained in those audiotapes, digitized over 2 years, we found 13 surviving recordings of 1968's "One Day in May," a monumental event on the Augsburg campus organized in response to national unrest as a result of systemic racism and the assassination of Dr. Martin Luther King, Jr. (see the chapter in this volume "One Day in May and the Fight for Racial Justice" for an in-depth exploration of this event in the life of Augsburg).[3] To work with archives is to know, and feel, what information you are missing and hold out hope that it will one day find its way home.

We have another woman of color to thank for helping us address a once-absent part of Augsburg's recorded history. The archives are home to an alternative set of yearbooks that began in 1987 when M. Anita Gay Hawthorne arrived on campus as Augsburg's new leader of the Office of Black Student Affairs (BSA). Now available online, these images are the bedrock of a collection that documents Black collegiate life over the past 35 years. In a way, their online versions are stills in a nonlinear motion picture that shows Augsburg's difficult—and ongoing—journey away from the grotesque mistakes of the mid-20th century. The collection provides clear evidence that we did not simply transform into a more diverse institution overnight. Instead, generations of people like Hawthorne struggled to make that change happen.

A graduate of Southern and Howard Universities with an impressive resume as a poet, Hawthorne brought a student-focused perspective and limitless energy to her new role. "I was not coming to Augsburg to fill anybody's shoes," she told *The Echo* shortly after she started; "I brought my own sevens" (Oliver, 1987, p. 7). In the first year of her leadership, the BSA office hosted more than 50 events, including holiday observations, art shows, speaker series, forums, poetry readings, open houses, church services, receptions, and workshops. Hawthorne did everything from serving homemade ice cream during Welcome Week to traveling to Nigeria as part of an Augsburg-affiliated visit (Hawthorne, 1988). By September 1990, in her role as advisor to the Black Student Union (BSU), she helped students change the BSU to the Pan-Afrikan Student Union (PASU) to be more inclusive of the entire African diaspora. It would take time for Augsburg to break out of its "culture cocoons," she said at the time of this important change, but she stressed, "we've got to learn how to make it work" (DeLong, 1990, p. 7).

The change worked thanks to the trust students placed in Hawthorne, whose focus on the entirety of the student experience helps explain why many Black students at Augsburg thought so highly of her that they called her "mom" (Hogan, 1998a, p. 19). Perhaps inspired by the familial role she played in students' lives, Hawthorne began to take photographs of them at PASU events and whenever they visited her office, much as a mother would document her family's growth. Her photography was especially prolific at commencement, where she took special care to document beaming students and the handful of Augsburg's Black faculty in their caps and gowns. At the end of each year, she assembled the photographs into albums that grew in scope as the years passed. By the mid-1990s, the albums had become careful records of Black staff, visitors, alumni, and others who are otherwise absent from recorded history at Augsburg. Even after Hawthorne's untimely death in 1997, Pan-Afrikan directors Brother Joe Young and Trena Bolden Fields continued the tradition of the albums until 2006, when born-digital photographs and social media took on the role of documenting student life. Taken as a whole, the albums amassed more than 5,000 images that are windows into the

lives of Augsburg's Black community during a time of growth and transformation. They also create a dialectic with the *Augsburgians*, inviting us
to consider Augsburg's saga from multiple, and sometimes conflicting,
perspectives.

In 2019, I began working with this collection when the Pan-Afrikan
Center's director at the time, Hana Dinku, came to the front desk of
Lindell Library and asked for me after hearing about my work digitiz-
ing Augsburg's archives, which began after Bill Wittenbreer retired. The
albums were located on bookshelves in the Pan-Afrikan Center director's
office, and there was little written context as to what they were, why they
were created, or who created them.[4] Dinku was interested in collabo-
rating with me and my team of student employees in Lindell Library's
Digitization Lab to preserve the images and make them available to the
community. It is important to note that approaching me (and thus the
institutional archives) was a leap of faith on Dinku's part. Archives have
a problematic history of "extractive" collecting approaches taken by predominantly white archivists who professionalized the seizure of cultural
artifacts, regularly made false promises of stewardship, and either put
items in glass display cases or hid them in dark rooms. I knew better than
to take that approach, but I could have made an equally poor choice in
simply claiming that I was too busy to be bothered, rejecting the immea-
surable historical value of the collection in favor of projects that piqued
my own interests.

Instead, Hana and I worked together to develop a plan for the Pan-
Afrikan Collection that specifically focused on the metadata, or the written information that describes each image so that they are discoverable
(Pan-Afrikan Collection, 2023). Metadata is at once professionally stan-
dardized and deeply subjective. The process used to describe archives
can determine whether their resources can be found or if they disappear
into the online equivalent of a dark room. We agreed that the metadata
needed to respect Hawthorne's original intent of the albums—to document the Black experience at Augsburg specifically. Thus, images that
showed Black people needed metadata that identified them as such. The
metadata also needed to recognize, elevate, and historicize the experiences of the Black community. I am grateful for the work of five student employees who undertook the painstaking process of scanning and
describing each photo, one at a time, over two years. Malia Abdullahi

'21, Henry Aryiku '21, Hannah Dyson '20, Clara Higgins '20, and Taiwana Shambley '21 contributed to the project and worked together to make this history come alive (Pan-Afrikan Collection, n.d.).

The albums are now located in the archives storage room, a 1,800-square-foot facility in the basement of Lindell Library that has been the repository of our institutional history since the Andersons moved the collection there in 1997. With rows of industrial shelving packed with yearbooks, literature, newspapers, magazines, record boxes, scrapbooks, posters, artwork, hanging portraits, and the odd groundbreaking shovel, it resembles a treasure room tucked into a cave that brims with knowledge and secrets. In one section, shelves laden with boxes, each full of DVDs, videotapes, and film reels, create walls of recorded memory, including a 1995 videocassette entitled "The Augsburg Culture." When played, the tape shows a grainy image of Carl Chrislock, longtime Augsburg history professor, and other elders telling stories. Chrislock credits another institutional historian, Gracia Grindal, for observing that Augsburg's culture is embedded with a sense of humor.

To illustrate this, Chrislock shared the story of teaching a course in partnership with St. Olaf College. The course had two sections, one held on each campus, and both included a guest lecture by Carlton C. Qualey, a historian of Norwegian immigrant history. Qualey's lecture included several anecdotes of, as Chrislock smilingly observed, "oh, um . . . financial—financial . . . misdeeds" by Lutheran clergy in the 19th century.

"Some of this was very funny," Chrislock remembered. "The Augsburg students [. . .] they just laughed! Thought all of this was very funny!" The same could not be said of St. Olaf's students, who reportedly frowned in silence (Chrislock et al., 1995, 37:41). This sense of humor has often reminded us, as Carl Chrislock put it, to maintain "a disposition not to take yourself too seriously" (Chrislock et al., 1995, 37:41). That humility is especially necessary for understanding the archives, where collections remind us that we have important, but small roles in an immense story.

Archives also remind us that we have limited control over the future, despite our most careful plans. Consider the sweeping architectural renderings of old campus master plans stored in large drawers in the archive's storage room. These plans, from our failed exodus to suburban "Augsburg Park" to a cringe-worthy proposal to replace Old Main with mirrored copies of Science and Sverdrup Halls, were lofty visions of futures that did not happen (Lang & Raugland, 1955). Some plans only materialized through a combination of hard work and sheer luck. Urness Tower, for example, is named for (and exists thanks to) Andrew and Mary Alice Urness, who surprised everyone when they donated $400,000 in 1966, though neither of them attended Augsburg nor even visited campus before their gift ("$400,000 gift," 1966; "Portrait of Urness," 1983; "Buildings dedicated," 1967).

Another example of divine serendipity took place in 1982, a few years after the Board of Regents prioritized making higher education accessible to students with physical disabilities—an immense task for campus structures built well before the Americans with Disabilities Act (ADA) became law in 1990. Development staff promptly organized the Making a Way Campaign, which raised $370,000 from American Lutheran Church congregations across southeast Minnesota to build ramps, accessible entrances, and elevators, making Augsburg the first private 4-year college in the Twin Cities to seek complete architectural barrier removal on its campus.[5] This effort included a unique gift from Fairview Hospital: a gently used skyway bridge, valued at $424,000, that Augsburg bought for a single dollar ("Accessibility," 1982; "Augsburg's leadership in accessibility," 1982). Moved across Riverside Avenue and installed between Memorial Hall and the Music Building (now Anderson Music Hall) in 1982, the world's cheapest skyway symbolized our commitment to providing education for all. It also testifies to our historically keen eye for a good deal.

Of many accessibility improvements funded by "Making a Way," one brings the story of the archives back to where they began. Architects initially puzzled over how to make Old Main accessible until they opted to tunnel into the building's basement, giving us the chance to pass by the original home for the archives. Campus buildings create their own kind of archive, giving us daily reminders that people dreamed of us as they struggled to make our work easier, our dorms more comfortable, our campus more accessible, and our time at Augsburg more meaningful (Augsburg University Archives, n.d.).[6]

The archives compel the paradoxes of our saga to share the same physical, digital, and conceptual spaces, overwhelming and challenging us in equal measure. On each shelf, within each box, in every absence, and through every online search, researchers will find sources of inspiration and pride interspersed with humility and even regret. Records of work by M. Anita Gay Hawthorne, Khin Khin Jensen, Mimi Baez Kingsley, Gerda Mortensen, Bonnie Wallace (Augsburg's first director of American Indian Services; see Eric Buffalohead's chapter in this volume entitled "Augsburg University Land Acknowledgement: A Case for More Than Mere Words" for more information about her important role), and many others remind us of the challenges that women and people of color have overcome at Augsburg, but they should also make us pause and reflect on why they had to overcome those barriers in the first place. We can celebrate Augsburg's diversity in the 21st century as we must understand the difficult path that led us to it. Even our campus, the physical testament to generations of generosity, is built on stolen land.

For nearly a century, archivists from Agnes Tangjerd to Kristin Anderson have worked to wrangle these historical contradictions together, at times without much financial support, let alone written recognition. Work in the archives is more than just putting things in boxes, scanning photos, or helping others write histories. Archivists are not idle caretakers of a graveyard. They are the stewards of living history, a garden that grows, blooms, and leaves behind seeds that wait for future sowing. The most difficult part of this work hinges on what to care for, what to weed out, and what to add. We cannot, and should not, save everything. What is important to remember? What can we forget? How do we decide?

Answers to these questions are still a work in progress. Our archives will continue to grow and change as the institution does, but they will always connect us to something greater than we could realize on our own. They are evidence of a love best expressed by M. Anita Gay Hawthorne in "From My Heart," a poem she wrote with Larry Bedford and recited in Hoversten Chapel in 1997 as her last gift to us ("M. Anita Gay Hawthorne's Epitaph," 1998):[7]

In the magic of the morning
When the day opens its eyes to mother earth,
Think of me . . .
I'll be thinking of you.

When the flaming sun shines down in
Radiance and sprinkles the glow over mother earth,

Smile for me . . .
I'll be smiling for you.

When the snowflakes fall
To cover with a white carpet mother earth,
Miss me . . .
I'll be missing you.

In the quiet of the night
As you close your eyes to rest,
Dream of me . . .
I'll be dreaming of you.

When we are apart from one another
Please know the loneliness I feel
And love me . . .
I'll be loving you!

Endnotes

1. This is an especially incredible gift considering that President Anderson was recovering from chemotherapy at the time.
2. "Naigrubsgua" is "Augsburgian" spelled backward.
3. See the chapter in this volume, "One Day in May and the Fight for Racial Justice" for more about this important historic event at Augsburg.
4. It is important to note that written context is not always necessary. The story of the albums was passed from one director to the next. Written documentation can be helpful, however, in keeping track of archival provenance, or the originating information of a collection.
5. The amount raised would be approximately $1.6 million in 2022, adjusted for inflation.
6. See the Campus Building Ceremonies Collection from the Augsburg University Archives (Augsburg University Archives, n.d.).
7. A separate version of the poem with an additional stanza was included in a memorial board created for Hawthorne ("M. Anita Gay memorial board," 1989).

References

$400,000 gift received from Mr. and Mrs. Urness. (1966, June). *Augsburg College Contact*, 7. Augsburg University Archives. Minneapolis, MN, United States. https://archives. augsburg.edu/islandora/object/AUGrepository%3A32837#page/7/mode/2up

Accessibility: From construction, improved attitudes, programs. (1982, March-April). *Augsburg College Now* 9. Augsburg University Archives. Minneapolis, MN, United States. https://archives.augsburg.edu/islandora/object/AUGrepository%3A34511 #page/11/mode/2up

Alburn, M. (1955, April 12). Educational TV near for Twin Cities. *Minneapolis Morning Tribune*, 1.

Area colleges to take part in first ED-TV telecasts. (1957, August 30). *The St. Cloud Daily Times*, 4.

Augsburg's leadership in accessibility for disabled students evident on campus. (1982 August). *Augsburg College Now* 12. Augsburg University Archives. Minneapolis, MN, United States. https://archives.augsburg.edu/islandora/object/AUGrepository %3A34498#page/1/mode/2up

Augsburg mourns loss of Spanish instructor. (1969, January 16). *The Augsburg Echo*, 1. Augsburg University Archives. Minneapolis, MN, United States. https://archives. augsburg.edu/islandora/object/AUGrepository%3A22091#page/1/mode/2up Augsburg University Archives. Minneapolis, MN, United States. https://archives. augsburg.edu/islandora/object/AUGrepository%3A32837#page/6/mode/2up

Augsburg University. (1930–31). *Augsburg Seminary Catalog 1930–31,* 26. Augsburg University Archives. Minneapolis, MN, United States. https://archives.augsburg.edu/ islandora/object/AUGrepository%3A42718#page/28/mode/1up

Augsburg University. (1940-41). Augsburg College and Seminary Catalog 1940-41. Augsburg University Archives. Minneapolis, MN, United States. https://archives.augsburg. edu/islandora/object/AUGrepository%3A43263

Augsburg University. *The Augsburgian 1948.* The Augsburgian Collection. Augsburg University Archives. Minneapolis, MN, United States. https://archives.augsburg.edu/ islandora/object/AUGrepository%3A620#page/1/mode/2up

Augsburg University. *The Augsburgian 1957.* The Augsburgian Collection. Augsburg University Archives. Minneapolis, MN, United States. https://archives.augsburg.edu/ islandora/object/AUGrepository%3A3681#page/166/mode/2up

Augsburg University. *The Augsburgian 1966.* The Augsburgian Collection. Augsburg University Archives. Minneapolis, MN, United States. https://archives.augsburg.edu/ islandora/object/AUGrepository%3A2956#page/43/mode/2up

Augsburg University Archives. (2019, Mar 11). *Augsburg homecoming parade footage (1949)* [Video file]. Retrieved from Augsburg University Archives. Minneapolis, MN, United States. https://youtu.be/5_lA5rxp8Gw?t=560

Augsburg University Archives. (n.d.). *Campus Building Ceremonies Collection* [Video file]. Retrieved from Augsburg University Archives. Minneapolis, MN, United States. https://www.youtube.com/playlist?list=PLp3IfZjFdUQJ5867g BvFOW7M5xvLLz3fl

Buildings dedicated at '67 homecoming ceremony. (1967, December). *Augsburg College Contact*, 8. Augsburg University Archives. Minneapolis, MN, United States. https://archives.augsburg.edu/islandora/object/AUGrepository% 3A32993#page/1/ mode/2up

Chrislock, C. (1969). *From fjord to freeway: 100 years, Augsburg College*. Augsburg College.

Chrislock, C., Sulerud, G., Johnson, E., & Johnson, M. (1995). *The Augsburg culture* [Video-cassette]. Augsburg University Archives. Minneapolis, MN, United States. https://youtu.be/Q5aYM791SVk?t=2261

Cosmopolitan Club hosts foreign students. (1954, October 6). *The Augsburg Echo*, 2. Augsburg University Archives. Minneapolis, MN, United States. https://archives.augsburg.edu/islandora/object/AUG repository%3A20673#page/2/mode/2up/

DeLong, R. (1990, September 28). PASU urges social change. *The Augsburg Echo*, 7. Augsburg University Archives. Minneapolis, MN, United States. https://archives.augsburg.edu/islandora/object/AUG repository%3A26328#page/7/mode/2up

Evenson, L. (1968, January 10). Archives tells history of Augsburg. *The Augsburg Echo*, 3. Augsburg University Archives. Minneapolis, MN, United States. https://archives.augsburg.edu/islandora/object/AUGrepository%3A21977#page/3/mode/2up

Fall enrollment up. (1960 , September). *Augsburg Contact*, 4. Augsburg University Archives. Minneapolis, MN, United States. https://archives.augsburg.edu/islandora/object/AUGrepository %3A32521#page/4/mode/2up

Hawthorne, M. A. G. (1988). *Black Student Affairs Calendar 1987–88*. Augsburg University Archives. Academic Dean Records (Box 3), Augsburg University Archives, Minneapolis, MN, United States.

Hogan, J. (1998a, Winter). M. Anita Hawthorne dies — "Mom" to Pan-Afrikan students. *Augsburg Now,* 19. Augsburg University Archives. Minneapolis, MN, United States. https://archives.augsburg.edu/islandora/object/AUGrepository%3A35538#page/21/mode/2up

Hogan, J. (1998b, Spring-Summer). Archival revival: Charles Anderson volunteers to organize college's history. *Augsburg Now*, 4. Augsburg University Archives. Minneapolis, MN, United States. https://archives.augsburg.edu/islandora/object/AUGrepository %3A35586#page/5/mode/1up

Hunter, J. (1956, June 15). Takes time out for a baby, then passes her PhD test. *The Capital Times*, 14.

Jensen Kantar, M. (2018, August 6). Honoring a pioneer woman Asian historian in the Twin Cities: Dr. Irene Khin Khin Jensen. *Middle Ground Journal*, 16. https://middlegroundjournal.com/2018/08/06/honoring-a-pioneer-woman-asian-historian-in-the-twin-cities/

Krohn, M. (1940, November 20). Dust reigns in old attic museum. *The Augsburg Echo*, 1. Augsburg University Archives. Minneapolis, MN, United States. https://archives.augsburg.edu/islandora/object/AUGrepository%3A19503#page/1/mode/2up

KTCA to start new series of programs. (1959, September 11). *The Minneapolis Star*, 13a.

Lang, A.I., & Raugland, O. (1955). *Plan for Augsburg College, circa 1955* [Photograph]. Augsburg University Archives. Minneapolis, MN, United States. https://archives.augsburg.edu/islandora/object/AUGrepository %3A44262

"Latin from Manhattan" returns from extended Chilean leave. (1968, February 28). *The Augsburg Echo*, 1. Augsburg University Archives. Minneapolis, MN, United States.

https://archives.augsburg.edu/islandora/object/AUGrepository%3A22002#page/1/mode/2up

Locals. (1914, March). *The Augsburg Ekko*, 24. Ausgburg University Archives. Minneapolis, MN, United States. https://archives.augsburg.edu/islandora/object/AUGrepository%3A15360#page/27/mode/2up

M. Anita Gay Hawthorne's Epitaph [Video file]. (1998). Augsburg University Archives. Minneapolis, MN, United States. https://youtu.be/pSpnETXbzP0

M. Anita Gay Hawthorne Memorial Board [Photograph]. (1989). Augsburg University Archives. Minneapolis, MN, United States. https://archives.augsburg.edu/islandora/object/AUGrepository%3A148147

Nelson, R. C., & Wood, D. (2000). *The Anderson chronicles: An intimate portrait of Augsburg College, 1963–1997*. Kirk House Publishers. Augsburg University Archives. Minneapolis, MN, United States. https://archives.augsburg.edu/islandora/object/AUGrepository%3A47855#page/25/mode/1up

The New Building. (1901–2). *Augsburg Seminary Catalog 1901-2*, pp. 6–9. Augsburg University Archives. Minneapolis, MN, United States. https://archives.augsburg.edu/islandora/object/AUGrepository %3A40890#page/6/mode/1up

Oliver, G. (1987, October 2). Faces. *The Augsburg Echo*, 7. Augsburg University Archives. Minneapolis, MN, United States. https://archives.augsburg.edu/islandora/object/AUGrepository%3A25728#page/7/mode/2up

Pan-Afrikan Collection. (n.d.). Augsburg University Archives. Minneapolis, MN, United States. https://archives.augsburg.edu/pan-afrikan

Pan-Afrikan Photograph Collection. (2023). Augsburg University. https://library.augsburg.edu/ld.php?content_id=57033589

Party for the Greens. (1959). *Augsburgian*, 21. Augsburg University Archives. Minneapolis, MN, United States. https://archives.augsburg.edu/islandora/object/AUGrepository%3A2357#page/24/mode/2up

Portrait of Urness: One of faith, friendship and devotion. (1983, Fall). *Augsburg College Now*, 3. Augsburg University Archives. Minneapolis, MN, United States. https://archives.augsburg.edu/islandora/object/AUGrepository%3A34603#page/2/mode/2up

School activities at Augsburg [Video file]. (1948–1949). Augsburg University Archives. Minneapolis, MN, United States. https://youtu.be/5rXYonHe9Ds?t=499 [16]

Storlie, C. (1962, April 4). Spanish teacher is SPAN advisor. *The Augsburg Echo*, 3. Augsburg University Archives. Minneapolis, MN, United States https://archives.augsburg.edu/islandora/object/AUGrepository %3A21284#page/1/mode/2up

Sverdrup Library, Archives, circa 1955 [Photograph]. Augsburg University Archives. Minneapolis, MN, United States. https://archives.augsburg.edu/islandora/object/AUGrepository%3A44506

Tetzlaff, A. (2017, April 21). Augsburg says farewell to librarian Bill Wittenbreer. *The Augsburg Echo*, p. 1. Augsburg University Archives. Minneapolis, MN, United States. https://archives.augsburg.edu/islandora/object/AUGrepository%3A31253#page/1/mode/2up

Thoughts at random–From the editor's notebook. (1958, January 9). *The Winona Daily News*, 6.

Town toppers: Here's a look at: Mrs. Mimi Kingsley. (1958, September 23). *The Minneapolis Star*, 23.

What's in a Name: SMU's Evolution to the Cardinals. (n.d.). St. Mary's University of Minnesota. https://saintmaryssports.com/sports/2012/5/26/GEN_0526120311.aspx?path=gen

Winter Sports Day at Augsburg College and Seminary [Video file]. (1949). Augsburg University Archives. Minneapolis, MN, United States. https://youtu.be/6Loomt ntFmM?t=453

Leaning In:

• • • • • • • • • •

Augsburg's Place and Proximity

The two chapters that follow illustrate the tension that exists in exploring Augsburg University's place, both in its geography and its relationship to its neighbors. Augsburg is a place-based institution (Bouzard et al., 2023), located in one of the most diverse zip codes in the United States. Its commitment to place is evident in the university's curriculum, campus life, and community engagement. At the same time, Augsburg is located, as it has been for more than 150 years, on land that was stolen from Native peoples.

Professor Eric Buffalohead offers a helpful history of the Native people who originally settled the land where Augsburg is located, and he points to the several ways in which Augsburg acknowledges the history of this land. President Paul Pribbenow then explores how those who founded Augsburg came to occupy this land, likely with no acknowledgement of its previous residents, and how subsequent generations of Augsburg leaders came to understand their role as stewards of this stolen land.

In the midst of this tension, the saga group explored how activist and public interest attorney Bryan Stevenson's notion of proximity could be a helpful way of navigating the tension of stewardship and place. As Stevenson has written, "There is power in proximity. When you get proximate to people who are suffering, you can wrap your arms around them, and you will be empowered with the belief that you can change the world. This will allow you to change the world" (*The Exonian*, 2021). For Augsburg, place becomes a portal for embracing our proximity to our students, faculty, and staff, as well as our neighbors, who reflect a diversity of ethnicity, religion, and lived experiences. Proximity, then, challenges Augsburg to name the tensions, both historic and in this moment, that exist in the places we occupy. We lean into those tensions!

References

Bouzard, G., Clark, K., Pippert, T., and Pribbenow, P. (2023). *Radical roots: How one professor changed a university's legacy.* Myers Education Press.

The Exonian. (2021, February 21). Bryan Stevenson discusses proximity. https://the exonian.net/news/2019/02/21/bryan-stevenson-discusses-proximity-2

Augsburg University Land Acknowledgment:

• • • • • • • • • • • • • • • • • • • •

A Case for More Than Mere Words

Eric Buffalohead

Introduction

In 2019, Augsburg University began using the following Land Acknowledgement:

> Augsburg's spirit is propelled by a heartbeat that started long before us. That heartbeat was present before our founding, when the land where Augsburg today stands was stewarded by the Dakota people. The Dakota are the original inhabitants of this area, and they are still here today. We honor their wisdom about this place, their recognition that we are all part of the same creation. We share their sense of obligation to the larger community, including to future generations. (Augsburg University, 2019)

This statement is an important step in acknowledging the fact that the land that Augsburg University now occupies is the former home to people known as the Dakota. The university has occupied this location since moving from Wisconsin in 1872. In order to truly understand the importance of this Land Acknowledgement, one must begin by examining the history of land dispossession of the Dakota people in Minnesota.

The Eastern Dakota in Historical Perspective

The term Sioux has been applied by outsiders to a number of culturally related regional and dialectal subgroups who call themselves Dakota, Lakota, or Nakota. As linguistic evidence suggests, the ancestral homeland not only for the Dakota but for all the Siouan speaking people may have been the Central Mississippi River Valley (Wozniak 1978). Oral tradition of the Minnesota Dakota, however, speaks of how the ancestors of the Dakota once lived to the north of their 17th century location in central and northern Minnesota near the north shore of Lake Superior (Bray & Bray, 1976, p. 35).

When they were first encountered by the French in the early 1600s, the Dakota lived in several villages throughout Minnesota. Oral tradition tells of seven divisions of the tribe collectively known as Oceti Sakowin (Seven Council Fires). The seven original divisions were:

Bdewakantowan—Spirit Lake People
Wahpekute—Shooters Among the Leaves
Wahpetonwan—Dwellers Among the Leaves
Sissetonwan—People of the Fish Village
Ihanktonwan (Yankton)—Dwellers at the End
Ihanktowana (Yanktonai)—Little Dwellers at the End
Tetonwan—Dwellers on the Plains

These seven divisions describe village locations. The Oceti Sakowin were most probably village states, each politically independent, but capable of collective action during times of crisis. Intermarriage commonly took place between families living in separate villages, and these kinship ties served to unify the separate divisions.

Within the village setting, the Dakota appointed a head soldier called "akicita" to keep order in daily affairs. Each village also had a council of adult males and a chief messenger. During emergencies, additional akicita were appointed. The akicitas, along with a war chief, made up the tiotipi, or soldier's lodge. The soldier's lodge also helped to maintain order during the annual buffalo hunt. From the ranks of the tiotipi, four hunt chiefs were selected. They and other members of the tiotipi could destroy anyone's lodge who moved ahead of the group and frightened off the buffalo herd. Their authority, however, lasted only for the duration of the hunt (Howard, 1984, pp. 4–7).

Around 1640, French explorers and missionaries began to establish themselves among the Indian nations of the Great Lakes. They began to hear about a great nation of warriors who lived to the west of the Lakes. The Dakota were said to live in large fortified villages, engaging in periodic warfare with the Cree to the north, and Miami and Illinois to the south. Their houses were "cabins of deerskin" (Meyer, 1967, pp. 5–6). In 1660, the French explorers Pierre Espirit Radisson and Sieur des Groseilliers, along with Medard Chouart, met with representatives of the Dakota nation for the first time. From the description of the location left by these explorers, this historic meeting may have taken place at Lac Courte Oreilles in what is now western Wisconsin. Representatives from 18 Indian nations came together to observe a memorial for the dead. This observance included burial of the bones of the dead, eating together, smoking the Pipe, ritual weeping, gift giving, dancing, and games played between host and visitor nations. During the proceedings, eight "Sioux ambassadors" arrived, accompanied by two women each. The women carried wild rice, corn, and other grains as gifts from their own villages (Meyer, 1967, pp. 1–5; Howard, 1984, pp. 1–2).

Twenty years after the Radisson and Groseilliers visit, other French explorers arrived in Dakota country. Daniel Greysolon Duluth traveled to the west end of Lake Superior and up the St. Louis River. There he helped to negotiate a peace between the Dakota and Ojibwe. This peace agreement lasted for nearly 50 years. The following spring, Father Louis Hennepin and two companions traveled up the Mississippi River where they were met by a Dakota scouting party. According to Hennepin, they were taken to a village near Mille Lacs Lake (Anderson, 1984, pp. 33–35).

Hennepin and his party probably encountered what became known as the Bdewakantowan division of the tribe. They took their name from their summer village near the shores of Lake Mille Lacs in Central Minnesota. The Dakota name for the lake, Bdewakan, is translated as Spirit Lake. The Bdewakantonwan are also referred to as Isanyati, which means "village of the cutting stone." This term later became Anglicized as Santee to refer not only to the Bdewakantowan but also to the Sissetonwan, Wahpetonwan, and Wahpekute. Thus, "village of the cutting stone" and

"spirit lake village" both refer to village locations around Lake Mille Lacs
(Bray & Bray, 1976, p. 253).

The Period of Relocation and Trade

Before 1685, the Santee or Eastern Dakota were indirectly involved in
the French initiated fur trade with other tribes of the Great Lakes region.
The Dakota received some European trade goods through tribal neighbors whose villages were closer to French settlements. By 1685, however,
a temporary trading post was established on Lake Pepin in southern
Minnesota. By 1700, "Pelee Island" at the head of the lake became the site
of an annual trade fair. This was the beginning of a commercial relationship that developed between the Dakota and the French.

Trade between Indian nations had gone on for centuries prior to the
arrival of Europeans. Commercial fairs were held each year along the
James River in eastern South Dakota and at the Mandan villages on the
Missouri River (Anderson, 1984, p. 29). Dakota notions of trade took the
form of reciprocal giving. This form of trade brought articles from the
Plains, such as ponies, buffalo robes, and meat into the woodlands and
brought woodland products, such as wild rice and maple sugar, to the
Plains tribes. Trade fairs and annual gatherings of the seven divisions
of the Dakota continued throughout the 18th century. Sometime after
1763, when the British took control of the Great Lakes fur trade from
the French, an Englishman named Jonathan Carver came into Dakota
country and left a detailed account of his travels. His journal contains
a description of one such annual gathering of the Dakota nation, which
he referred to as a Grand Encampment. This Grand Encampment took
place in a Wahpeton village some 30 miles upstream from the mouth of
the Minnesota River. At that time, representatives from all seven divisions
of the Dakota assembled annually to discuss matters of mutual interest
(Meyer, 1967, pp. 15–16; Anderson, 1984, pp. 54, 60).

Sometime between 1700 and 1750, the four eastern divisions began
to live for longer periods of time on the prairies south and west of their
old woodland homes. Gradually they left their permanent villages at Mille
Lacs Lake, Sandy Lake, Cass and Winnebigoshish Lakes, Leech Lake, and
Red Lake in northern and northeastern Minnesota to live on the prairie
(Meyer, 1967, pp. 13–14). By the mid 1700s, the Eastern Dakota lived along
the Minnesota and Mississippi rivers in southern Minnesota.

As Pond (1908/1986) notes,

> The villages of the Bdewakantonwan were on the Mississippi and Min-
> nesota rivers extending from Winona to Shakopee. Most of the Indians
> living on the Minnesota above Shakopee were Wahpetonwan. At Big
> Stone Lake there were both Wahpetonwan and Sissetonwan; and at Lake
> Traverse, Ihnktonwan, Sissetonwan and Wahpetonwan. Part of the Wa-
> pekute lived on the Cannon River and part at Traverse Des Sioux. There
> were frequent intermarriages between these subdivisions of the Dakota,
> and they were more or less intermingled at all their villages. (p. 4)

Why did these Dakota transition from the woodlands to the prairie?
According to ethnohistorian Gary Clayton Anderson (1980), some historians speculate that the move may have been instigated because of Ojibwe
western migration that encroached on historic Dakota villages. This
hypothesis is supported by oral histories recorded by Ojibwe historian
William Whipple Warren, who documented Ojibwe elders recounting bat-
tles amongst Ojibwe and Dakota "in northern and eastern Minnesota and
western Wisconsin. These oral accounts suggest that the Dakota were
gone from the Mille Lacs region by 1736" (Anderson, 1980, pp. 18–19).

Other historians confirm that the Ojibwe and Dakota were indeed fre-
quently at war from the early 1700s until well into the following century.
Anderson (1980) argues, however, that the four divisions of the Santee
Dakota had already begun to leave the woodlands before the Ojibwe
arrived. By 1727, a permanent French trading fort had been built at Lake
Pepin to the south. That winter, 600 Dakota camped at the fort. In the
spring they left to attend an annual trade fair being held further south
at the French trading village of Prairie du Chien. It is possible, then, that
Dakota participation in the fur trade precipitated a migration south and
west (pp. 18–19, 24).

After extensive white contact, the political leaders of each Dakota
village included a chief, a chief soldier, and a principal man. The chief
soldier was quite often the brother-in-law of the Chief (Wozniak, 1978,
pp. 21–25). However, the tiotipi, or soldier's lodge, also continued to be a
political influence in Dakota villages. Fur traders and government officials
who dealt with the Eastern Dakota viewed a chief as one who exercised
complete authority over his people. The Dakota, however, operated in a

more democratic fashion. The opinions of all villagers were given equal weight in the process of decision making. If one man wished to present an argument to his fellow villagers, "he called a feast, feeding those men he wished to lobby and thus obliging them to listen carefully to his point of view" (Anderson, 1984, p. 175).

In their new location along the river valleys of southern Minnesota, the Dakota continued to participate in the fur trade. By supplying processed furs to the traders, the Dakota could obtain steel tools and weapons, processed cloth and blankets, glass beads, and other new materials. These items gradually replaced stone and bone tools, pottery, and fur robes. In other respects, the Eastern Dakota lived much like their ancestors had lived. For a part of the year, they still built and lived in bark house villages. Here the women planted, harvested, and stored their corn. They also fished, hunted deer, and gathered prairie vegetable foods, including different varieties of berries and a nourishing bulbous root called *tipsinna*. In the fall, the men went muskrat hunting and the women gathered a supply of wild rice. During the winter months, families broke into smaller groups and the men hunted deer. In the spring, many families went to a favorite sugar bush where they processed sap into maple sugar. When the season completed, they returned to their bark house villages, and after planting, planned for an annual bison hunt on the prairies to the west (Meyer, 1967, pp. 20–23).

The Period of Treaty Making and Land Loss

The first formal treaty between the Bdewakantonwan division of the Santee Dakota and the United States took place in 1805. The treaty, negotiated by Zebulon Pike, an American military officer, ceded approximately 100,000 acres of land around the confluence of the Minnesota and Mississippi Rivers to the American government. The circumstances surrounding the signing of this treaty suggests questionable legality. First of all, the process by which the Dakota arrived at group decisions, by discussion and consensus among villagers, was ignored. Chiefs had no more power to make decisions than anyone else, and yet, Pike solicited only "chiefs" to sign the treaty. Of the seven Bdewakantonwan chiefs present at this historic meeting, only two signed. Congress also waited for some time before ratifying the treaty, and when it was finally ratified, the $200,000 agreed upon for the land was reduced to $2,000 without the consent of the chiefs who had signed the original treaty (Black Thunder et al., 1975, pp. 5, 131; Meyer, 1967, pp. 24–25; Wozniak, 1978, pp. 8–9). However illegal the Pike Treaty may have been, it did provide American settlers with a foothold in Dakota lands.

The Treaty of 1837 between the Bdewakantonwan bands and the American government opened lands east of the Mississippi River to white settlement. A provision in this treaty allowed band members to be supplied with whatever goods they might need for a period of 20 years. Some 14 years later, the Treaty of 1851 resulted in further land loss not only for the Bdewakantonwan but for all the Eastern Dakota bands. This treaty was negotiated by the territorial governor of Minnesota, Alexander Ramsey, and the territorial delegate, Henry Sibley. Ramsey and Sibley had several reasons to believe that a new treaty could be successfully negotiated. Reports had been filtering in that there was widespread starvation among the Dakota and therefore, they might be ready to exchange lands for a dependable supply of food. In addition, there was increasing pressure to open up lands west of the Mississippi River for white settlement. Minnesota had become a territory in 1849, and 5,000 settlers were living along a narrow strip of land between the St. Croix and Mississippi Rivers. Given this difficult set of economic circumstances for the Dakota, the land hunger of white settlers, and the chance to make money themselves by negotiating a new treaty, Ramsey and Sibley pushed ahead.

The leaders of the Eastern Dakota bands who were most influential in negotiating the Treaty of 1851 were men who had either converted to Christianity or who had taken up farming under the influence of white missionaries. These men included Walking Spirit, hereditary chief at Lac Qui Parle; Mahpiya Wicasta, Walking Spirit's war chief; Maza Sa (Red Iron), a village chief; and Paul Maza Kute Mani, Henok Mahpiya Hdinape, Peter Big Fire, and Simian Awanyang Mani. The missionaries had their own reasons for persuading Dakota leaders to sign the treaty. They had come to believe the only way the Dakota would adopt Christianity would be to give up their communal lifestyle. Giving up a communal life meant adopting the family practices, farming methods, and ownership patterns of the whites. This would be accomplished more rapidly, they reasoned, if the Dakota held only a fraction of their land base (Anderson, 1984, pp. 179–183).

The treaty conference itself was held in the summer of 1851 at the village of Traverse Des Sioux on the Minnesota River. When the commissioners, Alexander Ramsey and Luke Lea, arrived, they had to wait 2 weeks before key members of the Sissetonwan bands came in from a bison hunt on the Plains to the west. Neither Ramsey nor Lea had much experience in political conferences. Earlier negotiators had generally followed Indian customs and traditions. Those who wanted to persuade provided those who listened with a communal meal. For Indian people, treaty conferences were social as well as political events. Ramsey especially lacked understanding of Dakota political protocol.

A treaty was finally agreed upon on July 23, 1851. Thirty-six village chiefs ended up signing the treaty, and an equal number, especially among the Sissetonwan and Wahpetonwan bands, never agreed to sign (Anderson, 1984, pp. 185–191). According to provisions of the treaty, the Eastern bands of the Dakota agreed to relinquish a large portion of their lands. This territory ran roughly from central Minnesota in the north to northern Iowa in the south, and from the Red and Sioux Rivers in the west to an undefined border on the east. The area to be set aside as a reservation included land from Yellow Medicine Creek to Lake Traverse. In return for the ceded land, the government was to keep $1,360,000 in the United States treasury for 50 years. Other benefits of the treaty included $10,000 for food provisions and $18,000 for education and farming. In addition, the bands were to receive $305,000 "hand money," as it was called, to open farms in support of their needs until the first year's interest on their money arrived. With the support of some of the missionaries and mixed blood Indians, the traders got several Dakota leaders to sign a document which became known as the "trader's paper." This paper pledged some $210,000 of the treaty money to pay traders for alleged past debts. Many of those who signed this paper later stated they were led to believe they were signing a second copy of the treaty (Anderson, 1984, p. 187).

Between the treaty signing in the summer of 1851 and actual ratification of the treaty in Congress, a complicated series of deals took place between rival factions of traders and politicians in the Minnesota territory. The end result cheated the four divisions of the Eastern Dakota out of a substantial portion of their treaty money. Most of the $90,000 the Bdewakantonwan bands were owed ended up in the hands of the fur trader and territorial delegate, Henry Sibley, and another fur trader, Alexander Faribault. In a similar manner, over $200,000 of the money that was to go to the Sissetonwan and Wahpetonwan bands ended up in the hands of Alexander Ramsey and Henry Sibley. Those leaders who protested what was going on, such as Maza Sa (Red Iron), were arrested and stripped of their chieftainship. In all, the Dakota got 7 cents an acre for their Minnesota homelands. Those who really profited from the Treaty of 1851 got away with what has been called a "monstrous conspiracy" (Anderson, 1984, pp. 191–99; Meyer, 1967, pp. 78–79).

By the summer of 1862, tensions between the Eastern Dakota, the federal and state governments, and the white settlers became so intense that war erupted. The aftermath of the Dakota War, or "Sioux Uprising" as it was and still is referred to, proved to be devastating for the Eastern Dakota. Looking back, many issues seemed to have reached a climax that summer that led to the war.

First, a deepening split had developed within Eastern Dakota villages. Those who wished to continue living in a traditional way resented those who became Christian converts and those who had taken up the white style of farming and dress. Farming itself was not so distasteful to the traditional faction; rather, it was the style of farming imposed on them by the missionaries and government agents. Each family group was expected to store surplus crops in root cellars rather than share with others as was customary for the Dakota. Traditional leaders saw this style of farming as a form of hoarding, an unacceptable value in Dakota tradition (Anderson, 1984, pp. 232–33, 246).

The split between the two groups deepened still further when a number of Dakota farmers started a separate colony. The Hazelwood Republic, as it was called, was founded in 1856 with the help of Stephen Riggs, an Episcopal missionary. All the Dakota living in the colony practiced farming, dressed like the whites, and learned to read and write in their own language. After the colony was established, colony members campaigned to become citizens of the newly founded state of Minnesota. Their petition was denied. Then in 1860, some members of the more traditional faction began to harass the Hazelwood farmers. Hayfields and stables were burned, cattle were killed, and open threats were made. These events led up to the breakup of the Republic in the spring of 1860 (Meyer, 1967, pp. 102–107).

Secondly, after the Treaty of 1851, a large influx of settlers arrived to take over lands held by the Eastern Dakota. In former times, relationships between the Dakotas and Euro-Americans had been quite friendly.

Traders and government officials had married into Dakota families and had generally respected the customs of the people. The German immigrants who arrived en masse to the New Ulm area were quite different. The first winter they arrived, they took over the gabled summer houses (tipi tanka) that Dakota families had built. They made fun of Dakota customs and refused to share food. For the Dakota, refusing to share food was the most indecent and uncivilized way a human being could behave (Anderson, 1984, pp. 240–245).

Thirdly, by the 1850s white men who lived near the Eastern Dakota were regularly taking advantage of Dakota women. The missionaries, Williamson and Riggs, even complained about the behavior of the newly appointed Indian agent, Joseph R. Brown. They accused him of molesting young Dakota girls. Little Crow, who took part in the Dakota War, and his brother, Big Eagle, complained that the sexual abuse of Dakota women by white men was a major source of their anger against the whites (Anderson, 1984, pp. 227–235; Meyer, 1967, p. 59).

Finally, the trust relationship that had existed between the Eastern Dakota and the federal government began to fall apart in the summer of 1862. At the Yellow Medicine Agency, Dakota leaders asked the traders to extend their credit because the expected annuities were late in arriving. One of the traders, Andrew Myrick, is said to have remarked: "So far as I am concerned, let them eat grass." He was later found dead, his mouth stuffed with grass (Anderson, 1984, pp. 250–251; Meyer,1967, p. 117).

This insult had become typical of the strained relations between the Eastern Dakota and Euro-Americans. Dakota leaders were aware that the traders and politicians had cheated them out of much of their treaty money. They knew that cheating had occurred but they were not that angry because money did not mean that much to them. Nor were they that angry about ceding much of their land. They had always been willing to share land. What really angered them was the unwillingness of the whites to share when they called themselves "kin." Their failure to keep their promises was the final insult for many Dakota (Anderson, 1984, p. 260).

The war actually began among the Bdewakantonwan bands. On a dare, a group of young Dakota men killed a white settler and his family. After the incident the men knew there was no turning back. They quickly enlisted the aid of the Bdewakantonwan chief, Little Crow. At first, Little Crow did not like the idea of going to war with the whites. Only gradually did he become convinced. Dakota war parties made their first attack on the Lower Agency, near present day Morton, Minnesota. Here the warriors won a victory over a platoon of soldiers sent out from Fort Ridgely. White settlements in the "Big Woods" and New Ulm area were the next to be attacked. In all, over 500 white settlers were killed.

The battle of Wood Lake changed the tide of the war as Little Crow and his men suffered a defeat. After the battle, those who took part escaped to the Dakota prairies. Other Eastern Dakota who had remained neutral during the fighting and those who had grown tired of the war formed a Friendly Camp that became known as Camp Release. General Henry Sibley and his soldiers came into the camp, took the people hostage, and proceeded to arrest 1,200 Dakota (Meyer, 1967, p. 123). Those who were arrested were taken to prisons set up in Mankato and Fort Snelling. Three hundred prisoners were condemned to death for their part in the war, and of this group, 38 men were publicly hanged in Mankato on December 26, 1862 (Meyer, 1967, pp. 125–127, 137).

In the aftermath of the war, Congress abrogated all treaties that were entered into between the federal government and the Eastern Dakota. The Dakota, whether they had participated in the war or not, were all denied any further benefits outlined in the treaties. Congress then appropriated money for the removal of these bands to the west (Meyer, 1967, p. 140). After the war, the Eastern Dakota became scattered in several directions. Some escaped to live with relatives in the Dakota territory, and others escaped to Canada. Still others who had been arrested were removed to Crow Creek in the Dakota Territory. Later, this group was removed again to Santee, Nebraska. It was not until the late 1880s that lands in Minnesota began to be returned to the Eastern Dakota bands. This process continued into the 20th century. Returned land exists today at Prairie Island along the Mississippi River, at Prior Lake along the Minnesota River, at Lower Sioux along the Minnesota River near Morton, Minnesota, and at Upper Sioux along the Minnesota River near Granite Falls, Minnesota.

Augsburg's Response

To the credit of Augsburg, the university did not wait until the Land Acknowledgement to begin to respond to the troubled history of the land currently occupied by the university. Beginning in the late 1970s, several steps were taken in order to address the needs of Native students at the (then) college.

One of the most important first steps was the founding of the now-called American Indian Student Support Program (AISSP) in 1978. The first director, Bonnie Wallace, identified several needs of the Native students, including help with financial aid and housing, identifying appropriate courses in which to enroll, and making the transition from high school to college for distinctly different Native student populations (those from the reservation, those from the suburbs, and those from the inner city). Additionally, Wallace identified a need for American Indian Studies courses to be taught on campus. Wallace's efforts ended up leading to the beginnings of an American Indian Studies program, which would eventually lead to the creation of a minor (1990) and major (2001). The creation of these courses showed a real commitment to the local and regional Native community. They also provided a much needed safe space for Native students where they could not only learn more about their own people but about Native nations from around the United States and Canada. AISSP has had the luxury of having three consecutive long-term directors in Bonnie Wallace, Cindy Peterson, and Jennifer Simon. This stability has helped grow a strong Native student presence on the campus, which led to the creation of a student organization, Augsburg Indigenous Student Association (AISA), and the establishment of a University Powwow. Other important contributions include variations of Native Student Day, which brings high school students to campus in order to familiarize them with the institution.

The aforementioned American Indian Studies (AIS) program began to really come together in 1990, when it became an official minor area of study. The courses that were offered centered around American Indian History and Culture, as well as Ojibwe Language. In 2001, AIS became an official major area of study for students attending the (then) college. Course offerings were expanded to include contemporary Native issues, Native representation in film and literature, community engagement, and, most recently, Dakota Language. The year 2003 saw the launch of the Native American Film Series, which highlighted Native filmmakers and introduced them to the Augsburg community. In 2006, the AIS successfully petitioned to become the Department of American Indian Studies.

This move spoke volumes to the surrounding Native community about the commitment of the university to Native people.

The most recent very important step the university has taken was the establishment of the American Indian full tuition scholarship. This scholarship will make it possible for even more Native students to attend the university and attain a Bachelor's degree. This support is vital for a community plagued by incredibly high dropout rates at all levels of education.

Augsburg's commitment to Native peoples and the Dakota is clearly evidenced in these positive steps. Our common cultural commitments to stewardship and sharing, and our commitment to the land acknowledgement, provides ample room to continue on this path of supporting and acknowledging the peoples whose land our institution uses.

References

Anderson, G. C. (1980). Early Dakota migration and intertribal war: A revision. *Western Historical Quarterly, 11*(1), 1–31.

Anderson, G. C. (1984). *Kinsmen of another kind: Dakota–White relations in the Upper Mississippi Valley 1650–1862.* University of Nebraska Press.

Augsburg University. (2019). *Land acknowledgement.* Augsburg University and Luther Seminary Office of Marketing and Communication. https://docs.google.com/document/d/1DUvBPI3sNAePwgDgqjlrfxhlxwmwdAtN5X_Nq9lFMmg/edit

Black Thunder, E., Johnson, N., O'Connor, L., & Pronovost, M. (1975). *Ehanna Woyakapi: History and culture of the Sisseton-Wahpeton Sioux Tribe of South Dakota.* Sisseton-Wahpeton Sioux Tribe.

Bray, E., & Bray M. C. (Eds.). (1976). *Joseph Nicollet on the plains and prairies: The expeditions of 1838–39 with journals, letters, and notes on the Dakota Indians.* Minnesota Historical Society Press.

Howard, J. H. (1984). *The Canadian Sioux.* University of Nebraska Press.

Hughes, T. (1969). *Indian chiefs of Southern Minnesota.* Ross and Haines.

Johnson, E. (Ed.). (1974). *Aspects of Upper Great Lakes archaeology: Papers in honor of Lloyd A. Wilford (Minnesota prehistoric archaeology)* (Series 11). Minnesota Historical Society Press.

Meyer, R. W. (1967). *History of the Santee Sioux: U.S. Indian policy on trial.* University of Nebraska Press.

Pond, S. W. (1986). *The Dakota or Sioux in Minnesota as they were in 1834.* Minnesota Historical Society Press. (Original work published 1908)

Wozniak, J. (1978). *Contact, negotiation and conflict: An ethnohistory of the Eastern Dakota 1819–1839.* University Press of America.

Generosity and Faithfulness:
• •

A Meditation on Why Place Matters for Higher Education

Paul C. Pribbenow

The intrepid Norwegian-American immigrants who founded Augsburg Theological Seminary (now Augsburg University) more than 150 years ago chose as the institution's founding motto a simple claim from the New Testament Gospel of John: "And the Word became flesh" (John 1:14, NRSV). This foundation made all the difference for Augsburg's abiding commitment to place at the center of its academic mission and public purposes.

Allow me to explain why. First is the theological claim in that simple passage. The Gospel writer points to an incarnational proclamation: God came into human history, lived among us, and loved the world. In theological terms, this incarnation is the ultimate act of generosity and fulfills a covenant promise first made in the Hebrew scriptures. In other words, in this passage from John, we proclaim that God is generous and faithful on the ground, in our midst, and in the places we inhabit.

There follows from this theological claim a very real practical guide to life in the world for God's people. If God has been generous and faithful to us, the only fitting response is for us to be generous and faithful wherever we are found. In this way, John 1:14 stands the test of time as a guide to Augsburg's deep commitment to place as a source of its mission and identity. Place matters for Augsburg as it lives out its academic mission in service to the public good. Augsburg believes that it is called to be generous and faithful in its place.

My teacher, Martin E. Marty, taught me that colleges are place-based communities (Marty, 2003). That is, they are native to a particular place. They are native to a particular environment and a particular set of values and practices that define the institution. And that means something for the way they live their lives; it means something for the ways in which they understand what it means to be faithful and generous with their place, values, and presence.

For Augsburg, being place-based means acknowledging that the land it occupies was stolen, seeking reconciliation with its Indigenous neighbors, and then tending to its place with faithfulness and generosity. Augsburg is located in a particular place—a neighborhood called Cedar-Riverside in the heart of Minneapolis, Minnesota—that has been its home for 150 years. It is a neighborhood of Native peoples and immigrants—currently, primarily Somalis and Ethiopians, but over the years Scandinavians (our founders), Vietnamese, Korean, and others. And with these native and immigrant neighbors we share in what I call the saga of our life as an urban settlement (Pribbenow, 2014).

What is a saga? My understanding of the concept of saga comes from research done by Burton Clark on what it is that creates a distinctive character and identity for colleges and universities (Clark, 1972). A saga is more than a story; all of us have stories. A saga is more of a mythology, a sense of history and purpose and direction told in vocabulary and narrative that accounts for a community's DNA, even its essence. A saga abides in the sort of people, programs, and values that define an institution.

Clark contends that not every institution has a saga. Sometimes the lack of a saga is a function of not being true to founding values. At other times it can be occasioned by a change of location or core mission; still other institutions have not found a way to link their pasts, presents, and futures in a coherent narrative.

Augsburg University's saga runs deep in the culture and meaning of our work together. An exploration of Augsburg's history surfaces several themes that are central to our saga: an immigrant sensibility shaped in an urban neighborhood, freedom through faith to ask tough questions and engage otherness, a moral commitment to providing access to quality education for all, and the vocational aspiration to be neighbor to and with each other (Augsburg College, 2008). Together these themes inform Augsburg's identity and its abiding commitment to faithfulness and generosity in its place.

These themes also provide the foundation for seeing Augsburg as a 21st century urban settlement, a place-based institution settled in a particular neighborhood seeking to serve its neighbors and neighborhood in mutually beneficial ways (Pribbenow, 2014). In fact, we have articulated our calling as a college in this way: "We believe we are called to serve our neighbor" (Augsburg University, 2024). In that simple formula, we name our commitment to the inextricable links between faith, education, place, and service to and with the people who live around us.

The novelist Wallace Stegner once wrote that the American psyche is in tension between what he calls "the boomers," those who go into a place, use it up, and then leave, and "the stickers," those who settle in a place and work to renew it and make it better (Stegner, 1992, pp. xxii, 4). Augsburg is committed to "sticking," to staying and settling in. At Augsburg, we accompany and settle alongside our neighbors. We pursue education in our place, equipping each other for lives of meaning and purpose. We welcome each other in our place, sustaining a community of hospitality and mutual respect. We love and are faithful to the place that has been our home for more than 150 years.

How do we live out this commitment to "sticking" in and with our place?

We begin with the wise words of poet and essayist, Wendell Berry, whose work I return to often for guidance. In his prose poem, "Damage," Berry writes:

> No expert knows everything about every place, not even everything about any place. If one's knowledge of one's whereabouts is insufficient, if one's judgment is unsound, then expert advice is of little use. (Berry, 1990, p. 5)

I sometimes think about this quote when talking with all the experts who are happy to offer their advice (for free and for a fee!) about running a college. Our responsibility as "stickers" is to have knowledge of our whereabouts, otherwise all the experts in the world will be of little use. If we don't know our place, our mission, and our history, how can we expect to enlist others in pursuit of our aspirations? We know and care about our whereabouts so that we can be generous and faithful.

There are three simple aspects of our whereabouts, three ways in which place matters, and in which faithfulness and generosity are practiced, that are at the heart of Augsburg's mission and identity.

Perhaps the central focus of our whereabouts is that wherever Augsburg University is found—in our neighborhood, in the city, or around the world—*our most authentic work is learning and teaching*. And the wonder of learning is that it involves acts of generosity and faithfulness in its every detail—from teachers who teach what they love; to students who seek to learn out of curiosity and passion; to texts that bear the wisdom of the ages for our reflection; to conversations that help us pay attention to the Word, to each other, and to the world.

One of the joys of my life at Augsburg has been teaching a senior seminar. In the classroom I witness the generosity of what educator Parker Palmer has called "the grace of great things" (1998, p. 107), the gathering of a community around important issues and problems—great things indeed! I think about a course I taught on homelessness and affluence and how students wrestled with issues of justice, compassion, and the social realities of inequity and people living with both too little and too much. These issues were both studied in the classroom and experienced in the neighborhood. And around these difficult issues, we found the grace of great things, the generosity of learning from and with each other, and the connection to our place in the world.

For the Augsburg community, the commitment to teaching and learning and the connection to place are grounded in our mission statement, wherein we say that, "an Augsburg education is shaped by our urban and global settings" (Augsburg, 2010). That mission is part of an historic narrative that led the college in the 1960s to view its urban location as an extended classroom and to choose not simply to be located "in the city" but to embrace what it means to be "of the city" (Chrislock, 1969, p. 235). This important distinction sets a foundation for curricular and co-curricular programs that see our place as central to our academic mission and experience.

A second aspect of our whereabouts is the way in which our neighborhood and city is *a place that demands our presence as neighbor*. This particular neighborhood—much different now than in 1869, when the

Scandinavian founders of Augsburg lived nearby—now calls for us to be neighbor to those of very different backgrounds. Despite the evolution of the cultural and social context of our neighborhood, democracy still is practiced in this place with our neighbors. Education still happens in this place with learners and teachers all around us. Engagement and service still are at the center of our lives with each other in this place. Sustaining this urban place, this urban environment, is an act of generosity and faithfulness—for our diverse neighbors, for our diverse selves, for the whole of creation, now and into the future.

One of my favorite programs at Augsburg is our Campus Kitchen. Campus Kitchen's core work is led by students who collect leftover foodstuffs from our cafeteria and area restaurants, prepare, and then deliver more than 2,000 meals a month to our neighbors. It is good and important work. What I have seen in the past several years, though, is that our students have not been content simply to stay the course. They have focused our attention on the important role that food plays in our lives— as sustenance for our bodies, as fellowship for our community, and as politics and economics in our neighborhood and world. And the results are staggering. Yes, thousands of meals have been prepared and delivered, but there are now also community gardens on the edge of campus that bring together neighbors and students and children, a Farmer's Market on campus that involves relationships with organic farmers from across the region, composting of leftover everything in the cafeteria, and most recently, the opening of a food pantry on campus for students who go hungry. Here is an example of generosity and faithfulness in our place, attention and respect and concern for all of us who inhabit this neighborhood.

Our presence here cannot be passive or defensive. It must embrace the challenge of an Indigenous place, loving and caring for the land, the river, the environment, and the people. Our late Augsburg colleague, Jay Walljasper, who served as a senior fellow in the Sabo Center for Democracy and Citizenship, quotes Mexican novelist Carlos Fuentes, who says, "The citizen takes his (sic) city for granted too often. He (sic) forgets to marvel" (Walljasper, 2006, p. 7). We are generous and faithful in our place when we don't forget to marvel at all that is being done in our midst and all that we are called to do in return!

A final aspect of our whereabouts is Augsburg's commitment to our broader role in what I call our *"public work,"* or the positioning of the work of the college community in the larger context of achieving social justice and community building. Higher education institutions long have privileged their academic missions and often have found ways to care for their immediate environs through student service and civic engagement programs. I argue, however, that a commitment to generosity and faithfulness in place demands more of us. It demands bringing our many resources (intellectual, moral, and human) to bear in strengthening our democratic institutions and civic life.

Our public work at Augsburg is best exemplified by our leadership in the "anchor institution" movement in the Twin Cities of Minnesota. Augsburg has come together with sister higher education institutions, major health care organizations, and regional public agencies to understand how our self-interests as institutions can combine to create shared value for the neighborhoods along the light rail transit line. We now are engaged together in shared purchasing to support local businesses, workforce development to encourage the hiring of local companies and individuals, and place making—working together to create healthier and more sustainable neighborhoods. The results thus far illustrate positive economic impact on the region, but perhaps more importantly they show an intentionality about how the place we share can be strengthened through our collective efforts. This is not charity; this is a network business model that serves all of us and at the same time creates a more robust and vital civic life.

Our ability to scale these sorts of place-based initiatives means that our underlying commitment to our place can be extended and made even more central to our work as a university. As former Rutgers University–Newark Chancellor Nancy Cantor pointedly challenges us, colleges and universities must be "citizens of a place, not on the side lines studying it" (Cantor & Englot, 2015, p. 75).

I'll end with another brief quote from Wendell Berry, who, a few years after writing "Damage"—when he clearly was skeptical of our abilities to care adequately for our places in the world— wrote "Healing" to point to a more promising way:

> The teachings of unsuspecting teachers belong to the task and are its hope. The love and work of friends and lovers belong to the task, and are its health. Rest and rejoicing belong to the task, and are its grace. Let

tomorrow come tomorrow. Not by your will is the house carried through the night. Order is the only possibility of rest. (Berry, 1990, p. 13)

"The Word became flesh" thus is both a theological and a practical claim for Augsburg University. In response to the many gifts we have been given, we ask how we can be even more generous and faithful in our whereabouts and place. We accompany and settle alongside our neighbors, even when we come from very different cultures, religions, and experiences. And together we are creating and sustaining a safer, healthier, more vibrant place where generosity and faithfulness abound. I think our founders would be proud.

References

Augsburg College. (2008). *The promise of Augsburg College* [Video]. Vimeo. http://vimeo. com/79100160

Augsburg University. (2010). *Augsburg University mission statement.* http://www.augsburg. edu/about/mission/

Augsburg University. (2024). *University leadership.* https://www.augsburg.edu/about/ leadership/

Berry, W. (1990). *What are people for?* North Point Press.

Cantor, N., & Englot, P. (2015). Reinventing scholar-educators as citizens and public workers. In H. Boyte (Ed.), *Democracy's education: public work, citizenship and the future of colleges and universities* (pp. 75–79). Vanderbilt University Press.

Chrislock, C. (1969). *From fjord to freeway: 100 Years Augsburg College.* Augsburg College.

Clark, B. (1972). The organizational saga in higher education. *Administrative Science Quarterly, 17*(2), 178–184.

Marty, M. (2003). *Remarks to the annual meeting of the Federation of Independent Illinois Colleges and Universities* [Unpublished]. Independent Illinois Colleges and Universities.

Palmer, P. (1998). *The courage to teach: Exploring the inner landscape of a teacher's life.* Jossey-Bass.

Pribbenow, P. (2014). Lessons on vocation and location: The saga of Augsburg College as urban settlement. *Word & World, 34*(2), 149–159.

Stegner, W. (1992). *Where the bluebird sings to the lemonade springs.* Random House.

Walljasper, J. (2006). *The great neighborhood book: A do-it-yourself guide to placemaking.* New Society Publishers.

From Either/Or to Both/And:

Augsburg's Journey to Interfaith Living

Paul C. Pribbenow

The Norwegian-Lutheran pioneers who founded Augsburg College more than 150 years ago to educate teachers and preachers for their immigrant communities likely would not have imagined that today, Augsburg, one of 26 colleges and universities affiliated with the Evangelical Lutheran Church in America, would be a leading institution in the interfaith movement. Some might even consider this fact an indication that the institution had turned away from its founding values and identity.

I would argue, however, that our journey to interfaith living in the 21st century has been possible precisely because we are a college of the Lutheran church, not despite of that heritage. Instead of the "either/or" dialectic that creates chasms between insiders and outsiders, we have embraced a "both/and" perspective that enables us to be both faithful to the tradition that shaped us and relevant to the diverse cultures and faith traditions that are present in what theologian James Wallis has called "the new America" (Wallis, 2016). In this chapter, I will describe the logic that has guided Augsburg on this journey to interfaith living. First, I will address why our Lutheran Christian faith tradition undergirds our commitment to interfaith work. I then will outline how we have undertaken our interfaith initiatives on campus and in the wider community. Finally, I will describe what we are doing across the university and beyond to live out our commitment to interfaith living in 21st century America.

It is my firm belief that our interfaith work at Augsburg is a clear example of how higher education must be willing to change and innovate in response to changing demographics, social expectations, and democratic values. Being both faithful and relevant is a challenge all of higher education must address as we equip our students for lives of meaning and purpose in the world.

Why? The gifts of our faith tradition

Augsburg University celebrated its 150th anniversary in 2019. Founded originally as a theological seminary in 1869, the college evolved over the decades to become a comprehensive university, defined by excellence in the liberal arts and professional studies, and serving more than 3,200 students in traditional undergraduate, adult degree completion, and graduate academic programs. Located in the heart of the Cedar-Riverside neighborhood in Minneapolis—one of the most diverse ZIP codes in the country and home to myriad immigrant communities, including the largest Somali community in the United States—Augsburg has become one of the most diverse private colleges in the country. More than 75% of our first-year undergraduate class in the fall of 2023 were students of color.

Augsburg also has deepened its student body diversity beyond racial and ethnic categories. Once a haven for students who hailed from the homogenous towns and churches founded by our Northern European, Lutheran ancestors, today Augsburg is an institution that welcomes students of diverse cultural and religious traditions. We no longer have the opportunity to assume that our students share our Lutheran faith, and yet we contend that our faith heritage remains critical to our mission and identity, providing a foundation of core values and practices that continue to shape our academic mission and community life (Adamo, 2019; Chrislock, 1969; ELCA, 2018).

In order to address the inherent tension between the diverse students we serve and the tradition that has shaped our identity, we need to return to our tradition and name the gifts that make us who we are. During a presidential sabbatical in 2012, I specifically explored those gifts (or charisms) of our tradition—gifts that make us relevant to the needs of the world. Five particular gifts of our Lutheran tradition emerged in my research:

- We have the gift of the theological concept of *vocation*—the belief that God calls us to lives of meaning and significance in the world. We believe that we are called as an academic institution to help students discern their callings and to equip them to live out those callings.

- We have the gift of *critical and humble inquiry*—the belief that, already saved through God's salvific act in Jesus Christ, we are freed to seek knowledge and understanding, to ask difficult questions, and to make education a central value of a faithful life. We are grounded in the liberal arts, academic freedom, and the search for truth among competing ideologies.

- We have the gift of *engaging the other*—the claim that God's diverse creation is good. We believe that we are called to embrace diversity and otherness, to learn from each other, and to build healthy communities.

- We have the gift of *serving our neighbors and seeking justice* in human affairs—the belief that God calls us into relationship with each other and that our neighbors, individually and collectively, demand our love and service. We educate for service and justice in the world.

- We have the gift of *semper reformanda*—the belief that only God is permanent and that all human forms are imperfect and in need of abiding and loving reform. We are well positioned to build institutions that embrace change and value sustainability (Pribbenow, 2013).

With these five gifts of our tradition articulated, we then began the important work of translating their relevance for our commitment to serving our students in the curriculum, co-curriculum, and community outreach. This work, we argued, was a form of "evangelism," sharing the gifts of our faith with all of our students. This evangelism was not about converting students to our faith, but rather was grounded in the belief that the gifts of our tradition are in fact relevant to the mission-based commitments of the university to "educate informed citizens, thoughtful stewards, critical thinkers, and responsible leaders" (Augsburg University, 2010).

This belief in the relevance of our faith tradition for our identity and mission is informed by the work of Darrel Jodock, emeritus professor of religion at Gustavus Adolphus College, one of our sister schools in the ELCA. Dr. Jodock has developed a schema that describes a continuum of institutional identities, where on one pole reside "sectarian" colleges and universities, those whose identity is grounded in a particular faith tradition that is privileged in the mission and work of the institution (Jodock, 2002). Leading examples of sectarian institutions include Wheaton College in Illinois or Liberty University in Virginia. On the other pole are "nonsectarian" institutions, where religion might be studied but is in no way a part of the identity or mission of the university. Public institutions would be prime examples of the nonsectarian model.

Between these two poles of institutional mission and identity, Jodock describes what he calls a "third path" institution:

> I would like to suggest that a Lutheran identity commits a college to a third path—one that is neither sectarian nor non-sectarian. Unlike the non-sectarian model, this third path takes a religious tradition very seriously and seeks to build its identity around it, exploring the riches of that tradition as part of its contribution to the community as a whole. But, unlike the sectarian model, it seeks to serve the whole community and in so doing is ready to work with people of other religious traditions—indeed, welcome them into its midst. The sectarian and the non-sectarian models avoid religious diversity, either by withdrawing from it or by minimizing and sidestepping it. The third model takes religious diversity seriously enough to engage and struggle with it, while at the same time remaining deeply committed to the importance of its own Lutheran tradition. Rather than an enclave or a microcosm, the third option is a well dug deep to provide something helpful for the entire community. (Jodock, 2002, p. 2)

Jodock's "third path" describes Augsburg's efforts to combine its particular faith tradition with an openness to critical inquiry, learning from others, and equipping our diverse students for lives of meaning and purpose, no matter their paths in the world. It is upon this foundation that we have built our commitment to interfaith living at Augsburg. As Augsburg emerita professor Martha Stortz has written, this stance allows us to claim that "Lutherans pursue this interfaith work because we are rooted in this particular tradition, one that is always in the process of reforming and one that is graced with a robust sense of epistemological humility (Stortz, 2016, p. 13). In other words, interfaith work is not a luxury for our Lutheran college, it is a necessity.

How? An organizing framework for interfaith work across the university and beyond

Having grounded our interfaith commitments in our Lutheran faith tradition, we then began to explore the form these commitments might take on campus and beyond. We were pleased to work with the Interfaith Youth Core (now, Interfaith America), an organization founded and led by Eboo Patel and committed to partnering with colleges and universities to ensure that interfaith work is integrated into all aspects of institutional life. A comprehensive audit of Augsburg's curriculum and co-curriculum, along with a survey of students, was conducted by IFYC staff in 2009–2010. Its findings were critical in our strategic planning to integrate interfaith work in the college.

One of the most important contributions IFYC made to our work was a threefold framework—labeled the Interfaith Triangle—for organizing our interfaith initiatives (Interfaith America, 2024). When the IFYC staff provided their analysis and recommendations, it was in the context of three key questions:

- How do students (and others) gain knowledge (and understanding) of other faith traditions on campus? Is the work embedded in the curriculum? Are there community rituals and conversations that enhance knowledge of both the institution's faith tradition and other faith traditions present on campus?

- How do students (and others) develop relationships with those of other faith traditions? Does the college community have a diverse array of faith traditions in its midst? If not, are relationships with those of other traditions possible in the surrounding community? How does the institution promote interfaith relationships on campus—in the classroom, residence halls, and elsewhere?

- How do students (and others) develop healthy attitudes toward those of other faith traditions? How are unhealthy attitudes challenged and reformed? How are healthy attitudes celebrated and extended?

This framework became both a set of criteria to audit the current state of interfaith work on our campus, and also a set of organizing principles to help set priorities for enhancing our interfaith work together. As the next section describes, our work over the past several years has focused on all three aspects of this commitment—building knowledge, developing relationships, and shaping attitudes toward the other.

What? Implementing our commitment to interfaith living at Augsburg

Our journey as a Lutheran university from either/or to both/and, our efforts to faithfully walk the third path, is well underway, though far from complete. In this section, I want to describe in broad strokes where we have focused our interfaith work across the university. I will not attempt to be comprehensive, but rather to offer a glimpse into the on-the-ground efforts underway in four areas: curriculum, campus life, institutional practices, and community engagement.

In the curriculum

We know that we cannot leave the challenge of interfaith living to chance. In an academic institution, the way to ensure that all students are introduced to a concept is to embed it in the curriculum. At Augsburg, all of our undergraduates take at least one required religion course. The course introduces all students to the gifts of our Lutheran Christian faith tradition. As our faculty reports, these classes populated with students of diverse faith and humanistic traditions quickly turn into interfaith conversations as students share how the concepts they are learning relate, intersect, and perhaps clash with their own beliefs. That, I believe, is what education is about.

In addition, we have committed financial and professional development resources to further integrate our interfaith efforts into our academic program.

- With financial support from the Council of Independent Colleges' (CIC) NetVUE initiative (Network of Vocation in Undergraduate Education), our campus ministry office has partnered with faculty and staff to build an interfaith module into our first year seminar, ensuring that students understand our interfaith commitments early in their college careers.

- We have created an Interfaith Scholars program, led by our Interfaith Institute faculty, in which 10 to 12 students of diverse faith backgrounds are selected in a competitive process to participate in a credit-bearing, year-long seminar that includes study of various faith traditions, relationship-building, and service learning opportunities in various faith communities.

- In partnership with Interfaith America and CIC, we also have provided professional development opportunities for faculty members—both those who teach sacred texts and those who are facing, perhaps for the first time, a religiously diverse classroom. We don't assume that faculty members are always comfortable with the religious diversity of their students and we support them in ensuring that their pedagogical strategies are appropriate for diverse students.

In campus life

One example of our firm commitment to our Lutheran faith tradition is our practice of daily chapel during the academic year. Certainly most of the attendees at these brief chapel services share our Lutheran and/or Christian faith, but we also have begun to include on the chapel schedule opportunities for interfaith rituals and explorations. Often these chapel gatherings are organized and hosted by Interfaith Scholars.

In addition, we have engaged faculty, staff, community partners, and our campus space planning efforts to support interfaith living on campus.

- Our residence life staff now receive orientation and training about interfaith issues.

- We have created dedicated spaces on campus for non-Christians to meditate and pray, including making our chapel space available for Muslim prayers on Fridays during the academic year.

- Our dining service provider has been a willing partner in responding to the dietary needs of students from diverse faith backgrounds, including providing late-night dining options for Muslim students who fast during the day during Ramadan.

- We have added a Muslim student advisor to our campus ministry staff, believing that it is a source of strength to ground our interfaith work in an office dedicated to the spiritual life of the community.

In institutional practices

Perhaps one of the most challenging areas of promoting interfaith living on campus has been how we embrace and respect diverse faith traditions in our institutional practices. One simple commitment is to be mindful of the calendar and seek to respect the religious holidays of other traditions. For example, we have changed our employee policies to allow faculty and staff to use flexible personal holidays for religious observances.

We also have engaged in important and sometimes difficult conversations about how to integrate the rituals of our Lutheran tradition with the needs of a diverse campus community. We still carry the cross in our commencement ceremonies, contending that the cross is a symbol of the tradition that makes us the sort of college we are. At the same time, we have begun to think differently about how we illustrate our commitment to diverse faith traditions by going beyond simply Lutheran Christian practices. For example, at our annual opening convocation for new students, we complemented the traditional Christian invocation and benediction with prayers and readings from several different religious and humanistic traditions. The impact of this simple change in practice was profound—both for new students who witnessed our commitment to honoring both our own tradition and those of others, and for long-time faculty members who were visibly moved by this embrace of our multi-religious community.

I will admit that this effort to ensure that institutional practices honor our interfaith commitments is fraught with complexity. Being both faithful and relevant is hard work. In this effort, we count on a community that is both generous and gentle with each other, knowing that we will make mistakes and counting on each other to both hold us accountable and forgive our failings.

In community engagement

Our experience of the past decade in seeking to honor our commitment to interfaith living has occasioned opportunities to take our work outside of the campus community as well. Right in our own neighborhood, local Lutheran congregations now partner with Muslim imams to host interfaith meals and service projects. The local Jewish federation has partnered with us to send our students to Israel for study trips. Our religion courses benefit from regular visits to non-Christian faith communities, extending our teaching and learning community throughout the city.

Perhaps most meaningfully, our interfaith work has been embraced by our Lutheran church body. We are now leading an effort across the colleges and universities of the ELCA to integrate interfaith living into their diverse contexts and missions. Lutheran congregations across the country are seeking counsel and support from Augsburg to help them learn how to live alongside neighbors of diverse faith traditions. National foundations are looking to Augsburg to develop programs to support interfaith conversations and projects in Christian churches across the country.

Finally, we are proud to have received national recognition for our work from President Obama, whose Interfaith and Community Service Challenge was launched in 2008. Augsburg's interfaith efforts regularly are noted among the most effective among colleges and universities around the country.

In 2019, we formally established the Interfaith Institute at Augsburg, which was led by its founding director, the Rev. Mark Hanson. The institute focused on ensuring that Augsburg's interfaith work was firmly established across the university. In 2021, this deep commitment to interfaith leadership, learning, and living was strengthened by the creation of the El-Hibri Professor and Executive Director of the Augsburg Interfaith Institute, made possible by the generosity of the El-Hibri family. The inaugural El-Hibri Professor, Najeeba Syeed, has built upon the leadership of Mark Hanson, and has responded to the challenge made by the El-Hibri family upon endowing her position. That challenge is to ensure that Augsburg's focus on religious pluralism as a force for good in the world is evident in all we do on campus, and that this model of interfaith leadership is amplified by sharing it with organizations across the United States and the world.

As we consider the future of our interfaith work, we are convinced that dialogue and service must be interwoven in all we do. We believe that what we learned through recent efforts to encourage interfaith dialogue with our neighbors is something we must do each day. We must seek to live side by side, day by day, on campus, and within our neighborhood. Interfaith living is what we must—and do—aspire to teach our students.

Our work at Augsburg is informed by the 20th century political philosopher and theologian John Courtney Murray, SJ, who writes:

> Barbarism . . . is the lack of reasonable conversation according to reasonable laws. Here the word 'conversation' has its twofold Latin sense. It means living together and talking together. Barbarism threatens when men cease to live together according to reason, embodied in law and custom, and incorporated in a web of institutions that sufficiently reveal rational influences. . . . Barbarism likewise strikes when men cease to talk together . . . when dialogue gives way to a series of monologues; when parties to the conversation cease to listen to one another. (Murray, 1960, pp. 13–14)

Murray's challenge is clear: How shall we recover our capacity for conversation—both genuine living *and* talking together?

I find further inspiration for this important work in the example of the late Henri Nouwen, a Roman Catholic priest who wrote a moving challenge for what we are called to be and do in our interfaith living:

> Hospitality is not to change people, but to offer them space where change can take place.
>
> It is not to bring men and women over to our side, but to offer freedom not disturbed by dividing lines.
>
> It is not to lead our neighbor into a corner where there are no alternatives left, but to open a wide spectrum of options for choice and commitment.
>
> It is not an educated intimidation of good books, good stories, and good works, but the liberation of fearful hearts so that words can find root and bear ample fruit.

It is not a method of making our God and our way into the criteria of happiness, but the opening of an opportunity for others to find their God and their way.

The paradox of hospitality is that it wants to create emptiness—not a fearful emptiness, but a friendly emptiness where strangers can enter and discover themselves as created free; free to sing their own songs, speak their own languages, dance their own dances; free also to leave and follow their own vocations. (Nouwen, 1975, p. 55)

This is a vision of faithful living and learning that shapes the sort of education we seek to offer at Augsburg University. This is what we believe it means to be faithful to the tradition that grounds mission and identity, and relevant to the changing demographics and needs of the world. We must prepare our students for lives in an interfaith world. The ability of today's students to successfully navigate their futures depends upon being able to navigate a world brimming with diverse people with diverse beliefs. That requires innovation and imagination from colleges and universities whose work is at the heart of a healthy and vibrant democracy.

References

Adamo, P. (2019). *Hold fast to what is good: A history of Augsburg University in ten objects.* Augsburg University.

Augsburg University. (2010). *Augsburg University Mission Statement.* www.augsburg.edu/mission

Chrislock, C. (1969). *From fjord to freeway: 100 Years Augsburg College.* Augsburg College.

Evangelical Lutheran Church in America (ELCA). (2018). *Rooted and open.* https://www.elca.org/Resources/Colleges-and-Universities#RootedandOpen

Interfaith America. (2024). *Interfaith triangle.* https://www.interfaithamerica.org/resources/the-interfaith-triangle/

Jodock, D. (2002). *The third path: Gustavus Adolphus college and the Lutheran tradition* [Unpublished paper]. Gustavus Adolphus College. https://gustavus.edu/faith/pdf/Third_Path_Article.pdf

Murray, J. (1960). *We hold these truths.* Sheed and Ward.

Nouwen, H. (1975). *Reaching out: The three movements of the spiritual life.* Doubleday.

Pribbenow, P. (2013). *Faithful and relevant: Five homilies on Augsburg's vision.* Augsburg College.

Stortz, M. (2016). Why interfaith work is not a luxury: Lutherans as neighboring neighbors. *Intersections, 44*(4), 9–20.

Wallis, J. (2016). *America's original sin: racism, white privilege, and the bridge to a new America.* Brazos Press.

Augsburg's Pedagogical Tradition:

Firsthand Experiences, the City as Classroom, and Co-creating an Academic Journey

Babette Chatman and Jenny L. Hanson

The Beginning

Augsburg University has long regarded experience as essential for deep and significant learning. With each academic revolution since Augsburg's founding in 1869 (Chrislock, 1969),[1] faculty, staff, and institutional leaders have embraced contemporary—and oftentimes ahead-of-their-time—evolutions in teaching and learning. When the first three presidents of Augsburg—August Weenaas, Sven Oftedal, and George Sverdrup—set out to create an educational plan for the newly established institution in 1874, they saw a fundamental interconnectedness between the congregations students were being educated to serve, the communities in which those congregations were found, and society more broadly (Helland, 1920, pp. 62–66). As they saw it, the educational goals and responsibility of the institution were not to shuffle students into an ivory tower, but to help students reach their potential in service to society more broadly (Chrislock, 1969).[2] Sverdrup in particular rebelled against the standards of other Norwegian-American theological institutions of the day that separated students from the people they were supposed to lead as ministers. Rather than be removed from communities,

Sverdrup instead proclaimed that students "should relate organically to the communities or congregations that they ostensibly serve" (Chrislock, 1969, p. 236). To this end, the faculty at Augsburg's beginnings recognized that education had to be practical as much as it was theoretical and theological (Chrislock, 1969).[3]

Perhaps inspired by a combination of Lutheran theology and reformation ideals, the personal experiences of the founders forged in the early years of the institution's relocation from Wisconsin to Minneapolis, the proximity to both Danish and Norwegian-American settlements, and the experiences of the faculty, many of whom were immigrants themselves, the founders and early faculty embedded these ideals of interconnectedness and service into the fabric of the institution in myriad ways. This early educational philosophy elevated experience, and the truth within those experiences, as superior to those presented by established institutions (of which they were becoming). Truth gained from experience was to be valued, not discounted, dismissed, or displaced.

In the beginning, the founders connected with area congregations and communities to understand their goals, values, positions, struggles, and needs. They embraced how these experiences of being proximate to our neighbors helped students build empathy and kept them in service to others, whether they were pursuing ministry or not. Over time, this created a culture within the university of tending to both intellectual and personal growth, with a strong emphasis on experience.

But how does an institution grow and not become the ivory tower it set out to counter? Augsburg's faculty and institutional leaders recognized that experience needed to be intentionally curated, and at times fabricated, to promote experiential learning and foster education for service to others. Beginning with the second academic revolution in the 1960s and continuing to what might very well be the beginning of the third in the present day, significant community experiences—which were at times problematic—were integrated into the curricular structure of the academy.

In the following, we describe two vital and historic Augsburg programs meant to cultivate student experience beyond the classroom: The Crisis Colony and City Service Day.

The Crisis Colony

As Chrislock (1969) outlines, the second academic revolution at Augsburg in the 1960s called for the institution to take "noble aspirations" and turn them into "effective action" (p. 235). Nationwide, institutions were thinking about how to do this and Augsburg was no exception. "Augsburg chooses to be of the city," declared Augsburg president Oscar Anderson in the April 1969 issue of Augsburg's magazine *Augsburg College Now*, describing the city as an "unlimited laboratory" where students could experience "firsthand" the realities previously only "implied from afar" by textbooks (as cited in Chrislock, 1969, p. 235). The realities of an emerging urban society in the mid-20th century presented the opportunity to lean into experience and service again, highlighting the founders' mission and values to connect students with the community through direct experience—although by this time the divide was not between would-be clergy and lay people, but between students predominantly from rural and suburban areas coming to learn in an inner-city environment. In the 1960s, Augsburg was a predominantly white institution with students from rural and suburban areas seeking an education in the city at a small liberal arts college.

Anderson's call to be "of the city" and to take education into the streets and neighborhoods was accompanied by a push for the institution to help make "urban civilization livable" (as cited in Chrislock, 1969, p. 235). One response to this call was the creation in 1969 of an off-campus student living-learning community that experienced multiple iterations named the "Crisis Colony." Designed by Dr. Joel Torstenson, a founding faculty member of the Augsburg Sociology department, along with a local pastor, Rev. "Joe" Bash, students in the Crisis Colony spent a term living or doing in-depth service and learning on the Northside of Minneapolis. In addition to attending seminars, students volunteered for local organization campaigns, learned from local community experts, and had individual community-based work assignments (Bouzard et al., 2023, pp. 29–30). While the use of the term "colony" could be viewed as problematic, the program designers used the term specifically to refer to a group of people who establish residence in an area, and who build intentional community together while navigating the crisis of difficult and dangerous times in hopes of identifying solutions to the problems they encounter (Bash, 1969).

In his history of Augsburg, *Hold Fast to What is Good*, Philip Adamo (2019) described the Crisis Colony.

> Their teachers were the people who lived and worked in the commu-
> nity. Sociology professor Gordon Nelson joined Torstenson in teaching
> the course, first in the summer session, then as a fall semester offering.
> Crisis Colony had all the immediate and immersive aspects of study
> abroad in a foreign country, but it was happening just across town. Stu-
> dents experienced another culture, and learned from that experience .
> . . Sociology students worked in the Plymouth Youth Center and "Fun
> Clubs" for children in the housing projects. Education majors led chil-
> dren's drama groups, tutored students at a shopping center, and even
> attended parent-teacher meetings." (p. 48)

Ardyce Dunn, a student who participated in the Crisis Colony, said: "We went in [to the Crisis Colony] thinking we would help the poor blacks, but we realized the people of the community did not need our services as much as we needed theirs. We were there to learn from them . . . There was no way we could have learned these lessons in school. The Crisis Colony made the material in textbooks suddenly relevant" (Bash, 1969).

Dunn's reflection is perhaps one of the most important lessons. Practical experiences framed to students as service, coupled with course material that may have seemed outside the realm of their lived experi- ence when encountered on the page, suddenly came together in a way that gave students a perspective they didn't even know they needed. Together with coursework, the experiences students had promoted and practically integrated the ideals of service in the world so integral to Augsburg's mission, and exposed them to people and experiences they might never otherwise have had.

The Augsburg Crisis Colony experiment would end by 1970 for two reasons, finances and safety for the students. Afterward, the Crisis Colony transformed into MUST, or Metro Urban Studies, which was the first academic program of the Higher Education Consortium for Urban Affairs (HECUA), a group of colleges and universities that provided expe- riential off-campus programs for students with a focus on social change. Even though the specific Crisis Colony experiment was short lived, it clearly was consistent with the values and vision that had been a part of

Augsburg from the beginning; it lives on today in Augsburg's firm commitment to the Cedar-Riverside neighborhood and the various ways that academic courses, student-run organizations like Campus Kitchen, and centers like the Sabo Center for Democracy and Citizenship are connecting with, learning from, and working alongside our neighbors.

City Service Day

The 1980s saw a push to increase community engagement in society more broadly, and especially among young people who were perceived as being more interested in MTV than any sort of civic engagement. Faculty and students alike across the country began to consider what it meant to be engaged in one's community. National organizations like Campus Compact and the National Society of Experiential Education (NSEE) were established and began to influence higher education trends around service learning and civic engagement (what today might be called place-based community engagement, or community-engaged learning). While experiences connecting coursework to experiences in and with the surrounding community had been afforded to some students at Augsburg through either their majors in Metro and Urban Studies, Sociology, or Social Work, or through involvement in HECUA and the Conservation of Human Resources Program,[4] there was a push to expand opportunities for all students to connect their classroom learning with experiences in the city. By the end of the 1980s, Augsburg students and administration were calling for more action and funding to support service learning (Littlefield, 1994).

Rising to greet this charge, the college hired Mary Laurel True as the community engagement director in the Center for Service, Work, and Learning (now The Sabo Center for Democracy and Citizenship and The Strommen Center for Meaningful Work). True sought to increase student engagement in the community by bringing it into the academic environment. Faculty development was a cornerstone of this work. In 1994, the office hosted an institute where faculty who were already onboard with service learning in the classroom could discuss what they were doing, and others could begin to plan ways to integrate experiences into their classrooms. An outcome of the workshop led psychology professor and then director of the Center for Faculty Development, Victoria M. Littlefield, to author a handbook, with contributions from other faculty and True, titled *Community Service-Learning at Augsburg College: A Handbook for Instructors.* The handbook outlined 10 principles for combining community engagement and classroom learning, examples for how to structure a course, and clear steps to aid in a successful community-engaged educational experience.[5]

With this momentum, True worked to embed service in the community into all first-year seminar courses. The aim was to engage all incoming students (first-years and transfers) in service projects in the Cedar-Riverside neighborhood and across the Twin Cities.

To kick off all students' collegiate journey, students would participate in a day of service, called City Service Day, spurring their engagement in the surrounding community and conveying to them the importance of civic engagement and community service from day one. This immersion experience seeded into the collegiate journey the ideals of both serving and learning from our neighbors. It was not a one-off photo op, but rather was intended to initiate students into the values of an Augsburg education, marked by service, leadership, and stewardship.

The first recorded day of service was held in 1997. As with many things in academia, there was likely a pilot of some sort in the preceding years, as some accounts place the first "Day of Service" at Augsburg even earlier (1994, 1992). Augsburg was an early example of this type of community commitment, with Hamline, Macalester, and even the U of M launching similar first-year experiences. True became the bridge between the neighborhoods surrounding Augsburg and the university, facilitating countless service-learning projects on City Service Day and throughout the school year. True also worked to aid faculty as they embedded community-based experiences into their classrooms. This work included not just making the connection between faculty and community groups, but also teaching faculty about what it meant to embed service and sharing ideas based on best pedagogical practices. Sometimes the experiences True helped faculty design were short service opportunities, while other times the experiences lasted a semester or more. This allowed Augsburg students to truly build lasting relationships with the community—mirroring the relationships that Augsburg, through True, had established with longtime community partners like the Brian Coyle Community Center, Mixed Blood Theatre, Seward Community School, and The Cedar Cultural Center.

City Service Day became City Engagement Day in 2018. True led the effort through 2019. In 2020, the COVID-19 pandemic paused City Engagement Day. Soon after, Mary Laurel True left the university. City Engagement Day did not reemerge when the university resumed normal operations. There are a variety of factors that likely led to the end of this 20-year effort. Perhaps it had become an unwieldy task without True; it is also possible that faculty and students sought a change, as student demographics at Augsburg had changed dramatically since the mid- 1990s, with different needs and previous life experience, and faculty became more interested in pedagogies of active learning, decolonizing the curriculum, and building inclusive spaces.

The shift in nomenclature from City Service Day to City Engagement Day is one example of a change in approach to the notion of "service." The change was made intentionally, as students, and some faculty, began to question the value of "service in a day" in two distinct ways. First, some worried about the connotation of the word "service" in this context implying a kind of saviorism. Second, the realities of a diverse, justice-oriented student population with very different world views and experiences than students in the mid-1990s demanded a different articulation of service for the common good.

Some students, in particular BIPOC students, reported feeling like the work being done on City Service Day didn't really help the organizations or their constituents in any meaningful way. Students were familiar with some of the organizations and to them, City Service Day highlighted a disconnect between the institution, faculty, and students. It would seem a well-meaning white institution, with white faculty, were merely masquerading the word "service" but not really doing the work with the community. After all, how does cleaning an office or moving boxes really help combat racism? Furthermore, communities of color repeatedly experience "well-meaning white folks" trying to "help"—leading some students to perhaps approach City Service Day with understandable trepidation, especially on their first day of college. Thus, there was an effort to recognize that the day was a moment to connect with the community, to engage, rather than to do any meaningful service.

In terms of the experience, students began to question the value of City Service Day. What had once served as a way to connect students with the community and to learn from it seemed to lose its meaning. Students began to question what they were doing and what they were learning. Reports from first-year seminar groups varied, with some reporting having a meaningful experience, while others shared feelings of discontent, like the efforts on one day were merely tokenizing the communities they entered, or that the work was menial and didn't matter.

For example, for a first-year student who grew up in an urban setting and was tasked with picking up trash by a bridge on their first day of college, the engagement was rather blasé. They'd seen trash before and the trash will be here again tomorrow, whether they pick it up or not. They questioned what was to be learned by doing the work.

While the goals of learning through experience and the value of service didn't change, Augsburg's demographics did, and it would seem the pedagogical remnants of the service learning movement had lost sight of a couple of key tenets: making sure the experiences were appropriate for the learner with challenging actions that required students to go beyond their current knowledge and experiences, and ensuring a clear sense of both what is to be done and what is to learned with mutual input (those being served, those serving; those being taught, those teaching). Students who were already connected, who already understood many of the issues and circumstances in the neighborhood, didn't find challenges in these activities, nor did they see them as particularly just activities. Adding to the complexity, students of color were primed to have lower levels of trust in institutions, lower levels of self-efficacy (something service helps to build), imposter syndrome, and often carried an expectation that the promise of Augsburg would be something different. The activities that may have once challenged our student population and given them a sense of self-efficacy now seemed almost patronizing. Arguably, the end of City Service Day was a result of a disconnect between what the faculty and institution were offering and what the students needed.

This would speak to pedagogical shifts that diverted faculty attention and left them ill-prepared to adapt to the lived realities of students, resulting in the loss of the ideals of service and learning. Goals for some instructors had been to simply introduce students to something new and diverse, and get them out into the neighborhood. Yet, service in multicultural settings with multicultural participants not serving as saviors requires something different, something that addresses the shared reality and the real problems of racism, injustice, and countless other "isms." The pedagogy of service learning is not learn it and forget it, one and done. It requires constant attention and it must evolve. This requires the constant development of teaching methods, and of the teachers themselves.

Whether The Crisis Colony or City Service Day, no one could have anticipated the radical impact of community exposure on the learner of the time. We must re-embrace the tenets of integrating service and learning and reposition the learning and service in meaningful ways that are more than just proximate to our student's experiences. This means amping up the challenge, returning to sound pedagogy, and recognizing that we will have to do work that challenges us in new and profound ways, including co-creating the academic journey with our students and asking what it means to be in service adjacent to students who may be serving in their own communities.This is perhaps a marker of a third academic revolution, a revolution that challenges the privilege of the very institutional structures that are offering education. It is a revolution that recognizes that lived experiences matter, and that there is not a one-size-fits-all model for education. There is value in true co-creation of educational experiences that adapt to the needs of students, present challenge and opportunity, and do the work to live up to our promises, even when it is hard or the path unknown.

Endnotes

1. In his seminal history of Augsburg, Carl Chrislock asserts the institution experienced two academic revolutions. The first occurred near its founding when secular institutions began integrating accreditation standards typically embraced by larger institutions, and the second in the 1960s when academicians sought to teach differently.

2. In the Interpretative Statement by the Faculty that accompanied the 1874 educational plan for Augsburg, the faculty wrote, "We believe that not a single one of the many nationalities in this country should lose its identity before having an opportunity to make a distinctive contribution to our evolving American culture" (Chrislock, 1969, p. 21).

3. The faculty-developed interpretive statement of the 1874 Augsburg educational plan critiqued the established theological tradition. They preferred a program that sought to educate "committed servants of the people," and held experience as a higher truth than those of aristocratic "book" smarts (Chrislock, 1969, p. 26).

4. The Conservation of Human Resources Project started in 1969. Created by Cal Appleby and directed by Wayne Nelson, the program offered extension courses in prisons and state mental institutions and hospitals.

5.   The ten principles as outlined in the handbook were:
    1.   An effective program engages people in responsible and challenging actions for the common good.
    2.   An effective program provides structured opportunities for people to reflect critically on their service experiences.
    3.   An effective program articulates clear service and learning goals for everyone involved.
    4.   An effective program allows for those with needs to define those needs.
    5.   An effective program clarifies the responsibilities of each person and organization involved.
    6.   An effective program matches service providers and service needs through a process that recognizes changing circumstances.
    7.   An effective program expects genuine, active, and sustained organizational commitment.
    8.   An effective program includes training, supervision, monitoring, support, recognition, and evaluation to meet service and learning goals.
    9.   An effective program insures that the time commitment for service and learning is flexible, appropriate, and in the best interest of all involved.
    10.   An effective program is committed to program participation by and with diverse populations (Littlefield, 1994).

References

Adamo, P. (2019). *Hold fast to what is good: A history of Augsburg University in ten objects.* Augsburg University.

Bash, E. (1969). *A Rationale for the Crisis Colony Approach to Education* [Unpublished Paper]. Joel St. Torstenson Collection, Urban Studies Department Records Augsburg University Archives. Minneapolis, MN, United States. https://archives.augsburg.edu/islandora/object/AUGrepository%3A158747

Bouzard, G., Clark, K., Pippert, T., & Pribbenow P. (2023). *Radical roots: How one professor transformed a university.* Myers Educational Press.

Chrislock, C. (1969). *From fjord to freeway.* Augsburg College.

Helland, A. (1920). *Three-part plan.* Augsburg Seminar Gjennum Femti Aar, 1869–1919. https://archives.augsburg.edu/islandora/object/AUGrepository%3A151093#page/70/mode/2up

Littlefield, V. (1994). *Community-service learning at Augsburg College: A handbook for instructors.* Augsburg College. https://web.augsburg.edu/sabo/CommunityService LearningAugsburgCollege.pdf

Augsburg's Students:

· · · · · · · · · · · · · · · · · · · ·

Protest and Loving Reform

Augsburg's student body has become one of the most diverse in the country over the past 15 years, and with that diversity has come an urgent concern that the university is committed to equity and inclusion. The good news is that in Augsburg's historic saga, there is ample evidence that Augsburg students have long been fierce advocates for equity and justice

The following two chapters illustrate two critical forms of student advocacy: racial justice and LGBTQIA+ rights. University archivist Stewart Van Cleve and 2021 Augsburg graduate Berlynn Bitengo (who served as student government president in her senior year) recount the story of "One Day in May," a university teach-in that occurred shortly after the assassination of Dr. Martin Luther King, Jr. in 1968. They then explore the arc of the important conversations and demands that were made in 1968 up until the early 2020s, when, after the murder of George Floyd in Minneapolis, the university returned to the themes of "One Day in May" and renewed its commitments to racial justice and anti-racism.

In the second chapter, Archivist Van Cleve shares the story of lesbian and gay students at Augsburg, who, beginning in the 1980s, began to organize and advocate for their rights, often facing community backlash. Lyra McKnight, a student at Augsburg in the late 1980s, shares her memories of those organizing efforts and compares those experiences with those of her daughter, who attended Augsburg in the 2020s. Taylor Foster, '12, also recounts his experiences as a queer student during a very different moment in Augsburg's history.

Combined, these two chapters offer a rich picture of a student body engaged in critically important efforts to live out Augsburg's commitments to justice and equity.

One Day in May:

· · · · · · · · · · · ·

Past and Present Struggles for Racial Justice

Berlynn Bitengo and Stewart Van Cleve

On the morning of July 20, 1967, the front page of the *Minneapolis Tribune* informed readers about an overnight eruption of civil unrest along Plymouth Avenue, a major thoroughfare in the city's Near North neighborhood. Under the headline, "Fires Set, Rocks Thrown in City Mob Outbreaks," it also reported on acts of rebellion that occurred throughout the city, including vandalism and shouting in the Seven Corners neighborhood ("Fires set," 1967). Local dailies around the state used words like "mob," "riot," or "renegades" to describe the city's Black population and extensive property damage ("13 jailed," 1967; "Fires set," 1967; McFarland, 1967; "Violence," 1967).

Reporters, the police, and city leadership were perplexed by what happened, but people who lived in the neighborhood were not. That afternoon, the *Minneapolis Star* quoted Black community leaders who offered perspectives on the incident's origins. Syl Davis, the director of a Plymouth Avenue youth community center named The Way, noted that little had changed since a similar night of insurgence happened on the street a year before. Neighborhood youth took it upon themselves to organize The Way immediately following that unrest, and the center received support from business and city leaders. This limited support, Davis noted, was unable to address the scale of the problems that led to yet another uprising on the northside. "Nothing has really happened to prevent what happened last August," he told the paper (Hobbs, 1967). Theatrice "T" Williams, director of the Phyllis Wheatley Community Center on the Northside, and Edgar Pillow, director of Hennepin County's antipoverty programs, further noted that the underlying problems of systemic racism required year-round attention and dedicated effort. Without it, they warned, additional uprisings were distinctly possible (Hobbs, 1967).

They were right. After two more nights of public defiance, Minneapolis Mayor Arthur Naftalin petitioned Minnesota Governor Harold LeVander to activate the National Guard, and more than 600 troops descended along Plymouth and other streets in Minneapolis and St. Paul. The Guard's occupation of the Twin Cities ended a period of civil rebellion not seen since the Teamster's Strike during the Great Depression, or again until the George Floyd uprising in 2020 ("Uneasy calm," 1967).

Part of rebellions that shook more than a hundred U.S. cities in 1967, at times referred to as the "long, hot summer," the Plymouth Avenue uprisings are remembered through conflicting accounts from local newspapers, available records from the local and federal police, and people who witnessed them firsthand (McLaughlin, 2014). While some local retrospectives on Plymouth Avenue refer to these events as spontaneous "riots," others interpret them as part of a revolution against systemic oppression (Marks, n.d.).

With a nation still reeling from that summer's rebellions, President Lyndon Johnson created an official commission tasked with determining their causes to prevent future unrest in the United States. After 7 months and 424 pages, The National Advisory Commission on Civil Disorders published a report that cataloged injustices throughout American cities. Known by the name of the Commission's chair, the "Kerner Report" stressed that Black Americans did not have equal opportunities to the same comfort and privilege that white people had enjoyed for generations. It concluded that a lack of action would lead to two American societies: "one black, one white, separate and unequal" ("National Advisory," 1968, p. 1).

If many political leaders ignored its conclusions, the report transfixed activists and thought leaders, including those on college campuses (Gooden & Myers, 2018). At Augsburg College, a sociology professor named Joel S. Torstenson was among those who considered the report a clarion call. In a March 1968 meeting with President Oscar Anderson and others, Torstenson helped shape the initial idea of a "super day" to look at the problem of systemic racism in Minneapolis specifically (Torstenson, 2004, p. 70). Augsburg would invite leaders from The Way and other community institutions to campus as speakers in a daylong conference. They agreed classes would need to be canceled to focus on the event, and this would require a vote of the faculty in their regular meeting. In the afternoon on April 4, 1968, Augsburg's professors voted to "approve enthusiastically the idea" and promptly referred it to a committee ("Augsburg college faculty," 1968).[1]

A nationwide shock happened hours after their vote. While visiting Memphis to support striking sanitation workers, Dr. Martin Luther King, Jr. was shot to death outside his room at the Lorraine Motel. Anger and despair erupted around the country, and the tragedy added even more urgency to the idea of the conference. As he addressed Augsburg's community in the daily chapel the day after King's death, President Anderson noted that there was a strong desire for the "Day in May," but observed that Black community leaders could decline in the midst of such sudden grief (Anderson & Christiansen, 1969, 2:36).

Over the next month, as a volunteer team of student leaders worked diligently to coordinate speakers and arrange the program, Anderson adopted a firmer tone. On May 8th, he wrote an open letter to the Augsburg community that made attendance at the event morally (if not officially) obligatory for all students, faculty, and staff. He framed One Day in May as a crossroads in Augsburg's identity as a Christian college, giving a stark choice between attendance as an acceptance of "racial prejudice and bigotry as our own" and a problem to be "dealt with seriously," or absence as a "declaration in favor of racism and indifference . . . in a time of crisis" (Anderson, 1968; Lammerset al., 1980, p. 8). Anderson's use of urgent language to compel participation in the event echoed rhetoric that surrounded Augsburg's approach to understanding systemic racism at the time. Flyers created by the One Day in May planning committee included bright red text that read "1968: Urban Emergency!" and promised to focus on "Augsburg's role in the metropolitan crisis" ("1968: Urban emergency!", 1968).

Held in the just-opened College Center (now Christensen Center), the day's events used new architectural amenities and technologies. The state-of-the-art loudspeaker system piped soul music to start the day, and microphone setups in each room allowed speakers' voices to be heard on loudspeakers. The microphones were also connected to reel-to-reel audio recorders so tapes could be made available for people who could not attend. A newly devised closed-circuit television project allowed overflow attendees to watch some sessions live on a television set (Linden, 1968, p. 3; "A perspiring," 1968). As the building did not have air conditioning (until 1975), even its balconies and front steps became useful features that gave much-needed places to enjoy some fresh air ("The College Center," 1964, p. 2).

When the morning music ended, a standing-room-only crowd gathered by windows overlooking Murphy Square to listen to the day's first speaker. She was, in the words of President Oscar Anderson, highly sought by the organizing committee and well-suited to kick off One Day in May. Lillian D. Anthony had recently started her work as the first director of the new Minneapolis Department of Civil Rights, after serving as director of the Neighborhood Youth Corps of Minnesota ("Youth corps," 1966, p. 19). Within minutes of her arrival, Anthony commanded attention for a speech entitled "What Can You Do?" (Anthony, 1968). Demonstrating a keen sense of humor evident throughout the 53-minute speech, she anticipated the audience's anxiety over Black identities during a time of transformation, noting that the words "Negro," "Afro-American," and "Black" were each in use at the time. *"What do you really want to be called?"* she asked, imitating a question white people regularly expected her to answer. "You know," she replied, "that's one of those changes you're gonna have to go through with us, 'cause we haven't decided yet!" (Anthony, 1968, 2:38) With that, she joined the audience in an explosion of laughter.

Anthony's speech wove humor, poetry, and sharply worded recollections of overt racism that pervaded Minneapolis in the 1960s. She noted her own difficulty finding an apartment in 1965 and shared her experience traveling with a white pastor to understand housing discrimination. When she indicated an interest in an apartment, the landlord told her it was already claimed, but when the pastor expressed interest, it was available (Anthony, 1968, 17:11). In another story, she recalled flying over a burning Los Angeles when the Watts Uprising began. Upon hearing a fellow airplane passenger exclaim "What do they want next? We've given them *everything!*" she replied, "We want everything you have, and evidently they intend to get it" (Anthony, 1968, 28:24). She concluded her speech by summarizing a short story by Taban Lo Liyong. It tells of Monkey and Python, who force each other to harm themselves to make their bodies conform to one another's expectations. At the end of the story, marking the end of Anthony's speech, the Dove called to them both to: "accept him, as he is. Accept him, as he is" (as quoted in Balogun, 1984, p. 49).

The next plenary speaker, Edgar Pillow, offered an interesting counterpart to the more revolutionary themes evident in other speeches. Entitled "Racism in Politics and Power," Pillow's speech offered perspectives honed from his years in public service working with, and as part of, government agencies in Minnesota (Pillow, 1968). As the director of the Hennepin County Office of Economic Opportunity and a board member of The Way, Pillow carefully established the challenges of change-making when social movements interacted with powerful government institutions.

In between the keynote and plenary speakers, One Day in May offered simultaneous sessions, each with morning and afternoon components. A panel titled "Sex and Racism" included Lilian Anthony as well as Mary Howard, a psychology professor at Augsburg who was the first Black woman to formally teach at the institution, and it focused on intersections of sexuality, gender, and race in the United States. "People or Property" addressed police brutality and the media's fixation on property damage, rather than the underlying social problems that caused it. "Christianity and Bigotry" included panelist Orpheus Williams, a Reverend of the Emmanuel Missionary Baptist Church, speaking with two white pastors on racism in church theology and practice. Last, "Our Forgotten Neighbors" focused on the experiences of Black and Native American residents of Minneapolis, with the latter brought into sharp focus by panelist Ada Deer.

As the last plenary session speaker, Mahmoud El-Kati encountered an audience that had already contemplated multiple perspectives and was, perhaps, exhausted.[2] As education director at The Way, El-Kati was experienced with meeting listeners where they were and set about carefully dismantling preconceived notions that undergirded white supremacy, as he simultaneously wove his personal experience as a Black man in America's educational system. "In the mountains of books that you read in school," he told the audience, "they haven't gotten them straight in sociology yet.

They're still creating terms: 'ghetto,' 'culturally deprived' . . . I never knew I was 'culturally deprived' until I left Harlem" (El-Kati, 1968, 29:53).

After El-Kati's speech, at the end of a long day, President Oscar Anderson joined history professor Carl Chrislock, education professor Einar Johnson, religion professor Phillip Quanbeck, Vice President of Development Ken Fagerlie, and religion professor Douglas Ollila as the moderator in a panel that asked students "Where do we go from here?" Within minutes, the group of white men in leadership was arguing with students about Augsburg's role in sustaining systemic racism. Students, who heard and read about the urgency of the problem for weeks, were disinterested in the time or complexities involved with solving it.

LaJune Thomas Lange (née Johnson), who was part of a small community of Black students at the time, and part of the One Day in May steering committee, took to the microphone and presented her frustration. "I am not gonna stand back and let these people say that we have to learn after we get out of Augsburg," she told the room of almost all white people. She continued:

> Now President Anderson will sit in his office and tell me he believes in Black power, and then he'll come out here and say that 'we don't know what to do,' 'we can't decide now,' and 'we don't want to move too fast,' and 'be peaceful' and all this kind of stuff. Now we've got to have at least some positive approaches to the problem. . . . curriculum can't change overnight. I think everybody is realistic enough to know [that]. But if the Board of Education, which has control over most people, can say that, by September, we will have books by Black people, Black Americans in the English classes, as required reading, that Malcolm X will have, with parental permission, . . . a day off for him, and to recognize the contributions of all minority groups, for all the schools, in Minneapolis, and Augsburg's the only four-year liberal arts college in Minneapolis with fifty percent of its teachers graduating supposed to be going out to educate, and they're not aware of this? You can't be doing the function that you're supposed to. ("Where do we go," 1968, 25:39)

For Lange and other students, One Day in May was much like the Kerner Report that helped inspire it. While campus leaders were eager to hear more about "the problem," they were incapable of responding to it.

Anderson's and the other men's tones also indicated they were irritated at being confronted with that truth.

Lange and others were undeterred. The following day, as "Students United for Reality in Education," they presented Anderson with a list of demands:

1. Minority history by a minority instructor as a required course for all students, with no salary restrictions. Also the inclusion of minority contributions in all other existing history courses.

2. A revised FAME [Financial Aid for Minority Education] program that will be structured by black students at Augsburg. Hire Afro-Americans and members of other minority groups as counselors, recruiters, and additional required personnel as specified in the FAME proposal.

3. Employ members of minority groups as student recruiters.

4. Employ members of minority groups as employment personnel for staff and faculty.

5. Immediate sensitivity training for all faculty and staff members by an accredited organization approved by minority students at Augsburg.

6. Revision of the Religion department's required courses to illustrate realistically today's role of religion in waging wars, the Weber thesis, and in the institutionalization of racism in America.

7. Employ a black or other minority member as a compliance officer for the enforcement of all contracts concurrent with Project Equality.

8. Purchase only multi-ethnic texts in history, sociology, education, art, and other areas wherever relevant, or by means of supplementary texts when necessary.

9. An elective literature course dealing with minority authors and their contributions to literature. In addition, a balanced emphasis of works by minority authors in required English courses.

10. Bookstore promotion of literature by black and other minority authors.

11. Realizing the concern and plans that have already been exhibited by involved faculty members and since Augsburg is an "inner city school," we want to further demand that Augsburg realistically train its teachers to be able to teach in the "ghetto schools." This must include both classroom training and practical experience prior to student teaching. We also want to require 5 credits of the student teaching experience to be in the "inner-city" schools (Students United, 1968).

As "Where Do We Go From Here?" ended, so did the last tape recorded that day. Someone placed it in a box, grouped it with the others, and delivered it to Sverdrup Library to be cataloged and made available in the audiovisual library for people who were unable to attend. Decades passed, technology changed, and the tapes, much like the story of One Day in May, entered a cycle of being forgotten, remembered, and forgotten again.

In 1977, Augsburg faculty organized a forum to review Augsburg's progress and failures in responding to One Day in May and Students United for Reality in Education's (SURE's) demands (Benson, 1977, p. 2). Two years later, to celebrate Oscar Anderson's retirement, the campus began to host Days in May, a carnival celebration in Murphy Square that became a cherished memory for alumni in the 1980s and early 1990s— one that invited criticism from some original attendees of One Day in May who were upset at what it had become. "It is no accident that One Day in May has been turned into a 'pig roast,' [a] game-playing event devoid of serious political discussion of racism," wrote Bobbi Lammers, Larry DeSantis, and Terry Radovich in an *Echo* editorial in 1980 (Lammers et al., 1980, p. 8). In 2002, the Augsburg Sociology Club sought to bring the spirit of 1968 into the 21st century and organized One Day in May Revisited, featuring panel discussions held in the same rooms where the original event took place. While the "Revisited" sessions retained a focus on anti-Black racism, they also included a session on LGBTQIA+ issues that was especially pertinent in the context of the newly named Queer and Straight in Unity (QSU) group.[3]

For 16 years, One Day in May had been forgotten. It wasn't until 2019, when the then new Director for the Pan-Afrikan Center, Hana Dinku, learned the history of Black students at Augsburg through one of her mentors, elder Mahmoud El-Kati, one of the speakers during One Day in May. As Dinku was learning more about the history behind the day, she also learned that very few people at Augsburg knew about the day and the contributions made by Black faculty, students, and staff. The year 2019 also happened to be Augsburg's Sesquicentennial.

One of the ways the university was celebrating its 150th anniversary was by releasing a book titled *Hold Fast to What is Good*, written by History Professor Phillip Adamo; the book "tells the story of Augsburg through ten objects that have played a role in Augsburg's history from 1869 to today (2019)" (Adamo, 2019). However, in the book, there was no mention of One Day in May, a day of "public acknowledgment," which "created a level of transparency and accountability that helped move Augsburg in the right direction," according to Dinku (Weirick, 2021). Due to the lack of knowledge and acknowledgment of the day, Dinku worked with other leaders at Augsburg to make One Day in May the theme of the 2020 Martin Luther King, Jr. Celebration at Augsburg. As Dinku shared the significance of the day with members of the university, the administration, along with the Directors of International Student Services, LGBTQIA+ Student Services, and Multicultural Student Services, worked with faculty member Leon Wang to create and promote a Sesquicentennial campaign about One Day in May.

When asked by John Weirick, "What do you hope is accomplished through the reintroduction of One Day in May?" Dinku responded,

> "My goal for this campaign was to help Black students understand and appreciate the battles fought by those who came before them. I want Black students and other marginalized students to know that we are a part of Augsburg history; we are not guests at this institution. When the whole Augsburg community understands this, we will see the kind of institutional changes that marginalized students, staff, and faculty have demanded for years." (Weirick, 2021)

The community received the 2020 MLK Celebration well. Leo O'Ryan, a contributor to *The Echo*, wrote, "The Black History Month showcase was both rooted in the past through former Black leaders and alumni and in our future through our Black students performing their truth. The current board did a phenomenal job of organizing this, and I encourage all to show up to PASU's future events" (O'Ryan, 2020, p. 6).[3]

Four months later, on May 25, 2020, George Floyd was murdered by Minneapolis police. The nature of his murder caused protests across the United States and around the world because for 9 minutes and 29 seconds, Derek Chauvin, one of the four officers at the scene, knelt on Floyd's neck, causing a lack of oxygen. The incident occurred less than 5 miles from Augsburg University. On June 4, 2020, the Critical Race and Ethnicity Studies (CRES) working group made their official demand to President Pribbenow and then Provost Karen Kaivola. The working group demanded the immediate creation of the Department of CRES. "The coalition felt that the murder of George Floyd made the need for this department an urgent matter as it would ensure a generational commitment by the university to provide resources and opportunities for students of color" (Escobar & Shambley, 2020, p. 3). During a virtual Town Hall meeting on June 9, 2020, President Pribbenow announced the immediate creation of the CRES Department. In the fall of 2021, the Critical Race and Ethnicity Studies Department was implemented. The department has a major and minor in Critical Race and Ethnicity and a concentration in Asian American Studies, Latin/x Studies, and Africana Studies taught by faculty of color. In April 2020, a decision was made that the theme for the 2020 commencement would be "68/20: One Day in May." Honorable LaJune Thomas Lange '75 and Mahmoud El-Kati, two leaders from the 1968 One Day In May, were awarded honorary degrees during the ceremony.

The work of the CRES working group was a continuation of the 10-point recommendations listed earlier by SURE members to President Oscar Anderson on May 16, 1968, a day after One Day in May. With the recommendations, SURE wanted "everyone to start facing the fact that there are deficiencies in the educational system at Augsburg and to educate in the context of reality and not ideology" (Students United, 1968). According to President Anderson, One Day in May was a significant moment for Augsburg:

> Much is at stake at Augsburg in your attitude towards and participation in "One Day In May." This day will show whether, as a Christian college, we accept the problem of racial prejudice and bigotry as our own and

are actually willing to begin dealing seriously with it or whether we are hypocrites, after all, with a deep racial bias. Your refusal to actively participate in "One Day In May" will be understood as our declaration in favor of racism, prejudice, and indifference in a time of crisis—no matter how much you say to the contrary. "One Day In May" will be, I believe, a great day at Augsburg because it will be a chance for us as an entire community to be open and honest about a disease which has infected us all, as well as a chance to demonstrate to the minority community that all of us at Augsburg want to get on with the cure. Let us begin with ourselves. (Anderson, 1968)

"Let us begin with ourselves"—a statement true in 1968, and perhaps even more true today as we commit ourselves to the abiding work of seeking truth to freedom—through reconciliation. At Augsburg, this is the work we are called to do together as we pursue justice and seek to build the "beloved community" that Dr. King proclaimed.

Endnotes

1.   The next meeting, held on May 1, included a motion to rearrange classes for cancellation, but the motion did not carry. It is unclear (at the time of this writing) how most classes were canceled that day, but it is possible that the Academic Dean, Ken Bailey, approved cancellations on a case-by-case basis.
2.   Historical records of El-Kati's speech refer to him as "Milton Williams," a name he used at the time.
3.   See the "One Day in May Revisited Collection" in the Augsburg University Archives.

References

13 jailed in clash traced to wig fight. (1967, July 20). *The Minneapolis Star*, front page.

1968: Urban emergency! (1968). [Digital Image]. One Day in May Collection, 1968. Augsburg University Archives. Minneapolis, MN, United States. https://archives.augsburg.edu/islandora/object/AUGrepository%3A130850#page/1/mode/1up

A perspiring audience… (1968). [Photograph]. *The Augsburgian, 1968*, 45. Augsburgian Collection. Augsburg University Archives. Minneapolis, MN, United States. https://archives.augsburg.edu/islandora/object/AUGrepository%3A4771#page/48/mode/2up

Adamo, Phillip. (2019). *Hold Fast to What is Good*. Augsburg University. https://www.augsburg.edu/150/order-the-Augsburg-history-book

Anderson, O. (1968, May 9). *Letter from Oscar Anderson Declaring One Day in May 1968*. One Day in May Collection. Augsburg University Archives. Minneapolis, MN,

United States. https://archives.augsburg.edu/islandora/object/AUGrepository%
3A130859#page/1/mode/1up

Anderson, O., & Christensen, B. (1969, April 5). Augsburg chapel service [Audio file].
Augsburg University Archives. Minneapolis, MN, United States. https://youtu.be/
jdeV7lFWP2Q [8]

Anthony, L. D. (1968, May 15). What can you do? [Audio file]. One Day in May Collection.
University Events (Reel-to-Reel) Collection. Augsburg University Archives. Minneapolis, MN, United States. https://archives.augsburg.edu/islandora/object/AUGre
pository%3AODIM-

Augsburg College faculty meeting minutes. (1968, April 4), 1. Faculty Records UA 0531,
folder Faculty Meeting Minutes, 1966 to 1968. Augsburg University Archives. Minneapolis, MN, United States.

Balogun, F. O. (1984). Characteristics of absurdist African literature: Taban Lo Liyong's
fixions—A study in the absurd. *African Studies Review 27*(1), 41–55. https://doi.
org/10.2307/523949

Benson, A. (1977, April 29). Augsburg's promise to abolish racism set for forum review. *The
Augsburg Echo*, 2. Augsburg University Archives. Minneapolis, MN, United States.
https://archives.augsburg.edu/islandora/object/AUGrepository%3A23554#page/3/
mode/2uEl-

The College Center is one step closer to being air-conditioned! (1964, November 8). [Photo-
graph with caption]. *Augsburg Echo*, 2. Augsburg University Archives. Minneapolis,
MN, United States. https://archives.augsburg.edu/islandora/object/AUGrepository
%3A23011#page/3/mode/2up

El-Kati, M. (1968, May 15). Racism in education. [Audio file]. One Day in May Collection.
Augsburg University Archives. Minneapolis, MN, United States. https://archives.
augsburg.edu/islandora/object/AUGrepository%3AODIM

Escobar, C., & Shambley, T., Jr. (2020, September 18). Augsburg creates new Critical Race
and Ethnicity Studies Department. *Augsburg Echo*, 3 Augsburg University Archives.
Minneapolis, MN, United States. https://archives.augsburg.edu/islandora/object/
AUGrepository%3A130466#page/3/mode/2up

Fires set, rocks thrown in city mob outbreaks. (1967, July 20). *The Minneapolis Tribune.*

Gooden, S. T., & Myers, S. L. (2018). The Kerner Commission report fifty years later: revisit-
ing the American dream. *The Russell Sage Foundation Journal of the Social Sciences,
4*(6), 1–17.

Hobbs, M. (1967, July 20). Negro leaders foresaw riot. *The Minneapolis Star.*

Lammers, B., DeSantis, L., & Radovich, T. (1980, May 9). And everybody thought it was a
pig roast. *The Augsburg Echo*, 8. Augsburg University Archives. Minneapolis, MN,
United States. https://archives.augsburg.edu/islandora/object/AUGrepository
%3A24309#page/1/mode/2up

Linden, P. (1968, May 1). Sheep brains, actors, wrestlers all on CCTV. *The Augsburg Echo*,
3. Augsburg University Archives. Minneapolis, MN, United States. https://archives.
augsburg.edu/islandora/object/AUGrepository%3A22017#page/3/mode/2up

Marks, S. (n.d.) *Civil unrest on Plymouth Avenue, Minneapolis, 1967*. MNopedia, Minnesota Historical Society. http://www.mnopedia.org/event/civil–unrest–plymouth–avenue–minneapolis–1967

McFarland, R. (1967, July 20). Race Riot Extends to Minneapolis. *The St. Cloud Daily Times*, front page.

McLaughlin, M. (2014). *The long, hot summer of 1967: Urban rebellion in America*. Palgrave MacMillan.

National Advisory Commission on Civil Disorders, 1967. (1968). *U.S. Department of Justice Office of Justice Programs*. https://www.ojp.gov/ncjrs/virtual-library/abstracts/national-advisory-commission-civil-disorders-report

One Day in May Revisited Collection. (2002). Augsburg University Archives. Minneapolis, MN, United States. https://www.youtube.com/watch?v=I0RZOS8MVVU&list=PLp3lfZjFdUQI–lsBLJz23_eM1qupAbye8.

O'Ryan, L. (2020, March 6). PASU builds community with Black history month showcase. *Augsburg Echo*. 6. Augsburg University Archives. Minneapolis, MN, United States. https://archives.augsburg.edu/islandora/object/AUGrepository%3A129207#page/7/mode/2up

Pillow, E. (1968, May 15). Racism in politics and power. [Audio file]. One Day in May Collection. University Events (Reel-to-Reel) Collection. Augsburg University Archives. Minneapolis, MN, United States. https://archives.augsburg.edu/islandora/object/AUGrepository%3AODIM [18]

Students United for Reality in Education (SURE). (1968, May 16). SURE Letter to Oscar Anderson, 1968. One Day in May Collection. Augsburg University Archives. Minneapolis, MN, United States. https://archives.augsburg.edu/islandora/object/AUGrepository%3A130875#page/1/mode/2up

Torstenson, J. (2004). *Takk for Alt: A Life Story* (R. Torstenson, Ed.). Self-published.

Uneasy calm prevails on N. Side. (1967, July 22, p. 1). *The Minneapolis Star*.

Violence comes to North Minneapolis. (1967, July 20). *The Fergus Falls Daily Journal*, front page.

Weirick, J. (2021, January 29). On the spot: Hana Dinku. *Augsburg Now*. https://www.augsburg.edu/now/2020/08/28/on–the–spot–6/

Where do we go from here? (1968, May 15). [Audio file]. One Day in May Collection. Augsburg University Archives. Minneapolis, MN, United States. https://archives.augsburg.edu/islandora/object/AUGrepository%3AODIM

Youth Corps job to begin. (1966, January 20). *The Minneapolis Star*, 19.

Loving Reform and the Fight to Be Seen:

• • • • • • • • • • • • • • • • •

LGBTQIA+ Perspectives in Conversation

Stewart Van Cleve, with reflections by Lyra McKnight and Taylor Foster

To fit with the subject at hand, this chapter will take a queer approach to share stories about LGBTQIA+ history at Augsburg. I will establish some historical context in the neighborhood before two generations of alumni will write from their perspectives since 1987. Punctuating four decades, our experiences should invite the Augsburg community to reflect on how much we have changed and how much further we have to go.

And now, for the Queer Historical Context! Feel free to cue up some disco and release any glitter on hand.

Like us, Augsburg's Norwegian Lutheran founders had perspectives on gender and sexuality that took shape with (and against) the interconnected forces of class, ethnicity, race, and religion. Intimate homosociality, for example, flourished between Norwegian Lutheran men at Augsburg for the first third of our history. This "friendship," "fellowship," or "brotherhood" permitted men to forge deep physical and emotional relationships and express them in public without their affections coming under immediate scrutiny or an impulse to categorize it.[1] One photograph in the archives shows this clearly. In it, men hold hands and put their arms around each other as they attend chapel service in Old Main during the 1920s (Adamo, 2019, p. 128).[2] It is certainly not how I pictured a Christian service during that time!

Homosocial intimacy was not exclusive to men. When Gerda Mortensen, Augsburg's first Dean of Women, recorded a series of oral histories for the college's 100th anniversary in 1969, she noted women leaders in higher education "never dreamed that we could be Deans of Women and be married [to men] at the same time," adding "it was sort of a call to [a] commitment of life to that kind of service" (Mortensen, 1969a, p. 12). That commitment helps us understand how she described her friendship with Marian Lindemann, a French professor and Mortensen's close friend for decades. As she sat with Lindemann to record her oral histories, Mortensen recalled their first meeting and stressed the impact she felt personally:

> I shall never forget that entrance [of the] magnificent, beautiful woman made onto our campus and into our lives. And how she could like simple little me, I don't know. But she represented scholarship, refinement, culture, centuries of breeding, all this kind of thing. She brought into our society at Augsburg a quality of life that was more American than we were. We were still very much an immigrant people. And I think many of us reached out for this quality in our life. (Mortensen, 1969b, p. 14)

There is much more to learn about homosociality in this early part of Augsburg's history, but I am especially curious about its relation to a later era of queer repression in the Cedar-Riverside neighborhood. Packed with saloons, bars, and liquor stores frequented by Norwegians and other Scandinavians who were *probably not* attending chapel at Augsburg, Cedar Avenue was referred to—perhaps pejoratively—as "Snoose Boulevard,"[3] the writhing spine of one of Minneapolis' notorious "vice areas" before and after Prohibition (Westergren, 2006). In these areas, marginalized people aggressively contested social rules that enforced expectations of gender and sexuality (Schmid, 1937, Chart 195).

One of my favorite historical LGBTQIA+ images comes from the neighborhood during this period. In 1947, in an unidentified tavern near Cedar Avenue and Franklin Avenue, police arrested four young "female impersonators" for violating an anti-crossdressing law in the city that had been on the books since 1877. Instead of cowering in the shadows, the three white people and one Black person posed with defiant, ear-to-ear grins for *The Minneapolis Star*, which published their photo in the newspaper—along with their names and home addresses ("Female impersonators fined," 1947, p. 17).[4] Just up Cedar, one of the earliest known Minneapolis bars for queer and/or gender nonconforming women, The Holland, was a haven for women and sex workers in and beyond the neighborhood from 1956 to 1965 (Blade, 1993, p. 28; Twin Cities Public Television, 2017, 26:03).

By then, visible signs of Norwegian Lutheran homosociality had left Augsburg, and the college had taken a repressive turn. In a 1956 form that students filled out for their counselor's reference, under the heading of "Personality Adjustment," students could place a check next to the statement "I do not enjoy being with members of the opposite sex" as a problem that the counselor could help with (Augsburg College Student Personnel Services, 1956). As late as 1964, young women starting at Augsburg as first years were required to have their mothers sign a statement "authorizing where she might visit" and mail it directly to the administration (Mortensen, 1964). The latter example was, perhaps, influenced by fears about changes in the neighborhood and intended to keep young women away from places like The Holland. Public officials had identified the neighborhood as "blighted" or a "slum" for decades, but after many Scandinavian immigrant families and businesses had moved away or closed by the 1960s, the area developed an increasingly bad reputation (Minneapolis (Minn.), 1950; Danielson, 1966, p. 3).

One person's blight is another's idea of cool. With plenty of aging (and thus cheap) commercial buildings and deeply affordable housing, Cedar-Riverside transformed into the epicenter of antiwar activism and local radicalism, isolating Augsburg with something of a reputation as "God's Own Corner," a conservative island in a roiling countercultural sea (B. von Fisher, personal communication, August 2017). The college dipped a hesitant toe in these waters when alumnus Harlan Christianson led other faith-based leaders and laypeople to launch the Coffeehouse Extemporé on the second floor of a commercial building at 22nd and Riverside (known for many years as "Smiley's Point") in 1964 (Mattson, 1964, p. 2). Intended as an alcohol and substance-free place for local youth to have deep conversations and "spontaneous interaction," the "Extemp" moved between a succession of abandoned storefronts on Riverside and Cedar for the rest of the decade (Nystuen, 1980, p. 5). Much to the deepening horror of Augsburg's leaders, it became a magnet for hippies and earned a reputation as the center of drug traffic on the West Bank (Jordan, 1969, p. 1B).

It also became the cradle of the local LGBTQIA+ rights movement in May 1969, when Extemp regulars Stephen Ihrig and Koreen Phelps met there and indeed extemporaneously founded a new organization called "Fight Repression of Erotic Expression." Using the acronym F.R.E.E., their organization was the necessary first spark of queer political organizing in the Twin Cities. It led to the creation of major LGBTQIA+ community institutions, including Twin Cities Pride, within a few years of its founding (Halfhill, 1993; Phelps, 1993; University of Minnesota Libraries, n.d.).

In the first two-thirds of the 20th century, Augsburg's approach to the Cedar-Riverside neighborhood oscillated between isolation and awkward engagement. By the 1970s, the college began a more direct and deep understanding of ourselves as part of the neighborhood. At times, this led to troubled interactions, evident in a cringe worthy 1971 panel titled "Forgotten Minorities." In it, each panelist was supposed to speak on behalf of their "forgotten minority" category: physically disabled people; a recipient of psychiatric hospitalization; an advocate for the elderly; unhoused people; women; people with cognitive disabilities; poor people; Native Americans; Mexican-American communities; and "homosexuals" ("Forgotten minorities panel," 1971).

It was uncomfortable. Folks were expected to introduce themselves by speaking about "how they experienced their differences." One by one, each tried to answer the question, until a local gay activist took the microphone. Jack Baker was a former F.R.E.E. member who sued for the right to marry his husband, Michael McConnell, in a case that ultimately made it to the U.S. Supreme Court (*Baker v. Nelson*, 1971). When it came to his turn to speak on behalf of "homosexuals," he ignored the prompt. "I have a question," he began. "I don't know why we're all in here talking about difference and all. We're not different at all, we're all human beings. I think we ought to pass the mic[rophone] around to the audience so they can tell us how *they're* [author's emphasis] different. I find it very unproductive" ("Forgotten minorities panel," 1971).

With that, the room broke out in applause. It was one of many important moments for Augsburg as it learned, through trial and error, that if
you expect to interact with the neighborhood, you'd better be ready for
the neighborhood to interact with you. Such engagements led to many
mistakes, including a failed attempt by the administration to ban an
LGBTQIA+ community newspaper, the inimitable *Equal Time*, from campus newsstands in 1989 (Edstrom, 1989, front page). But in making such
mistakes, and learning from them over decades, Augsburg became a better neighbor. The institution's own experiential lessons in community
engagement continue to model the community-centered learning process
for our students. This knowledge has developed over time, as a direct
consequence of student activism, and through the difficult work of community building. We must acknowledge the people who worked, and still
work, to build the LGBTQIA+ community in, out, and around Augsburg.

Augsburg's Coming Out Story: (BAGLS: An Herstorical Memory Perspective)

Lyra L. McKnight, B.S., MSW

I didn't particularly want to attend. Branwen (my daughter and a current
Augsburg biopsychology student) invited me. I didn't have high expectations for the Augsburg Alumni Weekend for myself; none of my friends are
the homecoming or class reunion types, so they wouldn't be there. Most
of my professors had already retired. I was going this time to connect with
Branwen, and build new memories. I didn't realize that I would be back at
school, remembering memories of my undergraduate years at Augsburg
(1986–1990). In particular, this is Augsburg's "Coming Out" story, during
the academic year of 1987–1988.

As with all memories, my recollection is just that—my very own recollection. It has its flaws, its gaps, and its personal perspective. This is
my herstory, as I lived it—as I remember it. Friends, acquaintances, and
those I perceived on the "not paying attention" side or "the other side
of the fence" will likely recognize bits and pieces of these events. Other
memories may not be known, remembered, or agreed upon. Thus it is
with memory.

All decades have key events, key people, and key inventions that
highlight turning points in society. In my memories, the 1980s were filled

with women's rights. Sandra Day O'Connor was the first female Supreme Court Justice, and Sally Ride was the first U.S. female astronaut to enter space. George Orwell's book *1984* was being read with deepening concern alongside the positivity of growing technology. World Hunger and the Midwest Farm Crisis brought forth global awareness to the issues of food. Dance movies rocked movie theaters all over.

And then there was the AIDS epidemic.

AIDS first came to light in America in 1981. Homosexual men were showing symptoms including fever, fatigue, weight loss, and recurrent infections. Sounds pretty common, except it wasn't. It wasn't treatable. It was life threatening. The CDC identified AIDS and HIV, and America's penchant for stigma found a new focus: AIDS. It was linked to homosexual men. Then it was spread from bisexual men to women, and from women to perinatal infants.

Amidst this background, this small-town Iowa girl came to Augsburg in the autumn of 1986. It was her first time in the big city of Minneapolis, and she was coming with her eyes wide open and heart pounding for great adventures. I was that girl. (I also want to share that the first time I walked down Nicollet Avenue, I really did have a beret, and I really did toss it in the air. It was a true "Mary Tyler Moore" moment. I got dizzy looking up at the Foshay Tower, the tallest building I had ever seen in person. I almost fell flat on my back.)

My first year at college was "a whole new world." I learned how to ride a city bus, discovered incense, and expanded my Midwest diet to include Vietnamese egg rolls and fried rice. There was something else, too; something that I didn't quite understand. I liked boys. I had dated several, and one of them really made my heart pound. But there was a girl at Augsburg. I liked her, too. Hmmmm . . .

I read about the Kinsey Reports (1948) in a sociology class. Alfred Kinsey, "the father of the sexual revolution," created the Kinsey scale to demonstrate that sexuality does not fit into two strict categories: heterosexual and homosexual. People might be in between, they might move up and down the scale over time, or they might even be asexual. I fit somewhere in between. Bisexual was the label.

As I was exploring my self-identity, I came across a group of Augsburg students who were having hush-hush conversations about sexual orientation, discrimination, and the fear of violence. Being an academic institution, I believed that people within the Augsburg community were better informed and more temperate in their personal and political views about homosexuality. But the stigma of AIDS was rampant in the United States, and Augsburg was no exception.

I joined the group of students talking about concerns on campus. It was 1986 (or was it 1987?). One student's car was vandalized, another student was threatened with physical violence. Several were "outed." Something needed to be done to protect people of differing sexual orientations. We decided to start a student organization. A legitimate student organization, but there was a process. An application needed to be filed with the Student Government. The group needed a name. We chose BAGLS (Bisexual and Gay/Lesbian Students). We needed a sponsor from among the ranks of Augsburg professors, assistant professors, or administrative staff. The Augsburg counselor at the time (sorry, I forgot her name)[5] volunteered. We chose Dr. Edwina Hertzberg, Chair of the Department of Social Work, to champion our new group. We chose a social work professor over the campus counselor as a PR measure—didn't want anyone associating our group with "mental health issues"—which many were already doing.

There followed a backlash on campus. Students and staff both raised objections to our inclusion as a legitimate organization. Some told us that we should just "keep it behind closed doors." Others said that as a Lutheran college, Augsburg ought not to condone homosexuality; the Bible declares it a sin. Still others brought up AIDS. With AIDS, there was additional conversation about those of us who were bisexual. We "played both sides" so we were the ones responsible for spreading AIDS to the heterosexual community. Our BAGLS application became a volatile discussion point with some students; others seemed to express a sentiment of "do as you will, it doesn't affect me." The student government didn't want to vote, so they called for an open mic forum, to be hosted in the upstairs dining hall. The night of the forum, I came around the corner at the same time that some of Augsburg College's finest athletes came to the stairs from the other direction. They recognized me (although why they should surprised me at the time, as I wasn't part of a large or popular social pool). I know they recognized me, because as I started climbing the stairs, several of them looked directly at me, and then moved into a single file on the opposite side of the relatively wide staircase. We were all going up, but instead of the usual mass group, there was a single me on the right, and a single file of them on the left. Wow. I scared the football team—or was it wrestling?

(Let me extend the caveat that at the time, I recognized several athletes. That does not in any way give leave to stereotype all athletes as having a negative attitude toward either homosexuality or the student group. It is likely that some of them were just attending because someone else talked them into it; others might have been looking for more information. Still others may have been supportive, but were just going in single file because that's what the group was doing).

Our student government president opened the forum with incredible decorum and a call for temperate, thoughtful questions and comments. His use of *Robert's Rules of Order* was masterful. For the most part, students adhered to those guidelines.

But several students came forward with Bibles and a bit of fire and brimstone. The students who refuted our right to be a legitimate student group quoted scriptures, mostly from the Old Testament (it's against the law, and God will punish you) or secular law (state sodomy laws were being repealed in the 1970s and early 1980s, but stopped when AIDS hit the headlines. Sodomy is still illegal in 14 states as of 2022, including Minnesota).[6]

Those in favor of voting BAGLS in as a legitimate student organization had a more positive claim of support in the New Testament (Jesus loves everyone). Statements were made about social justice and equal rights for all.

Other students stated that it was okay if we met as a group, but we didn't need to be a legitimate student group. Nobody wanted to know about sexuality—that should be kept private. And others talked about AIDS. If BAGLS became a legitimate organization, Augsburg would be promoting illegal sexual behavior and spreading AIDS on campus.

By the end of the forum, people had been heard. Not everyone agreed, but there was no violence. It was an act of civil disagreement—not quite as demonstrative as Thoreau's civil disobedience—but demonstrable nonetheless, in its way.

The student government voted, and BAGLS was granted legitimate student organization status. We even got a budget. It might have been around $200 (I don't recall the exact amount). I do recall that we used some of the money to have a party that included Domino's Pizza to celebrate our victory. Most of the rest of the money went to purchase books on sexual orientation for Augsburg's Lindell Library.[7]

I was a member, then chair, of BAGLS for 3 years. During that time, our group talked about current events in the media, including the AIDS epidemic and social justice for people with different sexual orientations. We drew support from each other, and offered support to many who remained "in the closet" but wanted a hand to hold or a shoulder to cry on during times of stress or trouble.

In hindsight, I sometimes feel underwhelmed by what our group accomplished. But then I think about what we did, and I am encouraged that we took that step, and another step, and then another.

When I visited my daughter at the Alumni event in 2022, I was amazed to see how much our large/small steps had evolved in the 35 years since BAGLS and Augsburg "came out of the closet." I could not have imagined 35 years ago that not only would BAGLS have evolved into three groups supporting the diversity of sexual orientation, expression, and cultural diversities, but also included staff specifically for us. Meeting Tristan Crowell, LGBTQIA+ Student Services Program Manager, was heartwarming.

Meeting current students involved in these groups was both a humbling and a proud moment for me. I was welcomed with open arms by these students and by Tristan. I listened to their stories, and they listened to mine. Together, we bridged the generational gap to learn about new perspectives.

Thank you, Augsburg, for your continued support and tremendous progress with and on behalf of the Augsburg University community. I am filled with joy that I was a part of Augsburg's Coming Out story.

Augsburg University: Where Community Becomes Family

Taylor Foster

My relationship with Augsburg began long before I stepped foot on campus and was a student. It started with my mom attending as a student from 1985–1990. My mom graduated when she was pregnant with me, so you could say Augsburg is in my blood. My sister also attended Augsburg from 2005–2009. I proudly joined my sister and was a student at Augsburg from 2008–2012.

When my sister began attending Augsburg, I was 16 years old and recently had come out to my family as a lesbian. I had known that I was different from other girls all my life, but I grew up in the church and wasn't sure that speaking my truth would be accepted. I saw how the Bible and religion were used as a weapon against the queer community, and I assumed they would be used against me too. Fortunately, my sister supported me and invited me to Augsburg to visit. During my visit to Augsburg, my sister introduced me to multiple lesbian students on campus who were happy, out, and proud. We also attended a drag show hosted by the queer group on campus. They had students and local drag queens from the Gay 90s perform. It was my first time seeing drag queens and queer people, happily living as their authentic selves. To say I was obsessed is an understatement! I found drag queens inspiring and still feel the same about them today! The experience was filled with happiness, celebration, and for me, hope. I had never thought about going to college before that. High school was challenging, so I wasn't interested in continuing my education after graduating. However, after that experience, I knew if I went to college, I HAD to go to school at Augsburg. And so I did.

I started school at Augsburg in August of 2008. I was so excited to be in the city and on a campus where I knew I could be out and be proud. I attended a huge high school with over 3,000 students, but I only knew four other queer kids. Augsburg felt like a fresh start where I could find authentic community and support. I had the pleasure of living in what we called Urness the furnace! I lived on the 7th floor, and at the time, they had gendered floors where the odd floors were all girls and the even floors were all boys. Coming out to people can be a complicated conversation but is especially difficult when living in a dorm full of strangers with communal bathrooms. I was concerned that being a lesbian would make people uncomfortable. Conservatives have often used bathrooms as a place to police queer folks and make claims that we are predators. Although nervous, I came out to a girl on my floor from Colorado the first weekend. Her name is Lauren, and she became my best friend. Lauren was instantly supportive of me and reassured me that it was all going to be okay. It felt amazing to come out and be fully accepted right away. She single-handedly got me through my first year at Augsburg. My roommate was less supportive or accepting and wouldn't let my girlfriend sleep in our room when she visited. Lauren graciously let us sleep in her room whenever we needed. Everyone else on my floor was super accepting, and we got along incredibly.

During sophomore year, Lauren and I lived together in Mortensen Hall. We had two fantastic neighbors move in next door who became our best friends. One of them was a gay man named Dan, and I was so excited to find more community on campus. The four of us were inseparable from that point forward. During sophomore year, I put myself out there more and joined the LGBTQIA+ group on campus. It was called Queer and Straight in Unity, or QSU for short. I met and made friends with many more students who were out or allies on campus, and my world rapidly grew. QSU meetings taught me so much about the LGBTQIA+ community and how expansive it is. Specifically, I learned about transgender people for the first time at 19 years old. I couldn't believe how much I still had to learn, but I was grateful for the group and the opportunity to learn and grow. We also attended LGBTQIA+ conferences nationwide and even hosted some on campus. Conferences allowed us to meet other queer folks from all over the country, learn from them, and grow in community with them. Every time I returned home from a conference, I was excited to be queer, live authentically, and implement things we learned on campus to make it safer and more inclusive.

By the end of sophomore year, our core group of queer students and allies had significantly grown. We all wanted to live together or at least near one another. We decided to apply for special interest housing for our junior year. We put in an application and stated our special interest was to create a community full of LGBTQIA+ students and allies. People heard about it, and the interest grew from our core group of 8 to 10 people to 28 people, enough to fill an entire floor in Mortensen Hall. The school granted our application, and we had our floor. We named it "Everybody Loves Everybody," or ELE for short. Living on the floor surrounded us with immediate love and support. We hung out every day and night, rarely locked our doors so people could come and go freely, and someone constantly blared Lady Gaga. We quickly became family. We even had potluck dinners for major holidays for folks who weren't welcome at their families' homes or people whose families lived out of state.

TRIGGER WARNING: THE NEXT SECTION INVOLVES MENTION OF ASSAULT

The ELE floor was exactly what we all needed before we knew we needed it. Shortly after we moved in and were living the dream on the ELE floor, one of my close friends (and someone I still consider family) was assaulted on campus. Justin is a gay man whose style and beauty are captivating. He stands very tall, but that night was even taller because he was rocking these incredible purple heels. Justin was outside the dorm hall minding his own fabulous business and was assaulted by someone visiting another student. They attacked him and another person who stepped in to defend Justin. Justin was assaulted simply for being himself. This act of violence, this hate crime, shook all of us to our core. Augsburg, for years, had become this incredible, safe place for all LGBTQIA+ folks to be our authentic selves, and in an instant, everything changed. I worked for the Department of Public Safety (DPS) on campus. When I got to work a few hours later and learned about the incident, I rushed to the cameras to see if it was true. I didn't and couldn't believe what I was hearing. I wept as I watched the cameras show me how cruel the world can be to people like us.

I saw this as a call to action. I was determined to surround Justin with the love and support he deserved and to show him he wasn't alone. I created a Facebook event called "Stand Up Against Hate" and invited others from the ELE floor to join. The idea was for everyone to wear a different color of the rainbow each day of the week in support and solidarity with Justin and all LGBTQIA+ Augsburg students. Less than 2 days after making the post, the number of people interested or attending was over 600. I had no idea how much the community, the allies, and the administration would show up. The week was an outpouring of love and support. It became a beautiful group effort all around. Dan went to Target and bought t-shirts and hats with different colors to pass out to folks who didn't have the color we wore on that day. I will never forget what it looked like to see the cafeteria full of students wearing the same color clothing. It was such a beautiful visual representation of love and support. It brought tears to my eyes. During the week, there were rallies and prayer circles. We even did a "March for Equality" around the campus, dressed head to toe in rainbows to reclaim the space as safe and ours.

The following weekend, Justin bravely and beautifully put back on his purple heels and strutted his stuff outside. His bravery made me realize I can and should be brave too. Shortly after that, I came out as transgender and became the first openly transgender student on campus. I spent the remainder of my time at Augsburg advocating for transgender students. I spoke with staff and administration about the importance of pronouns, and they worked with me to get mine right. I became co-president of QSU, and we hosted the first-ever Transgender Day of Remembrance on campus. Transgender Day of Remembrance is a day to honor and remember the lives of transgender people that were taken by anti-transgender violence. I also got permission from the administration to change some campus bathrooms to gender-neutral ones for the day. At the time, there were only eight gender neutral bathrooms on campus, and I wanted to show how inconvenient it can be to find safe bathrooms for transgender students. Bathrooms have notoriously been places for violence or safety issues for transgender people, and I wanted to bring awareness to it. Some days I would try to run back to my dorm room between classes just to use the bathroom without fear. I wanted people to understand how much something we all do can cause so much stress for transgender people.

Senior year, we continued the ELE floor, but we doubled in size and had two floors now in Mortensen Hall. We were a group of over 40 students, and it was amazing! QSU that year got to host a drag show, just like the one that had inspired me to come to Augsburg all those years prior. It was terrific having the queens from the Gay 90s come; everyone had so much fun, as always! That year I was more involved with making everything inclusive for all students, and I spoke with the administration and asked them to change the language for the homecoming king and queen vote. It originally had "pick one of each sex," and I asked them to change it to gender identity. At that time, there were multiple transgender or gender-expansive students, and I wanted to ensure we all felt included in the vote. Somehow, I was nominated as one of the men to be homecoming king, and I was shocked. They usually use the picture from your student id for voting, but mine was of me pre-transition. The administration asked me if I had another picture I wanted them to use, and I excitedly gave them a picture of me wearing my new favorite bowtie.

They announced the homecoming king and queen at a pep rally in front of the whole school, and I feared what might happen. Even though I had an overwhelming amount of love and support at Augsburg, I was still terrified by the chance of being laughed at or made fun of in front of everyone. Much to my surprise, I not only did not get laughed at, but I won! I was up there with some of the most prominent athletes on campus, and they all cheered me on as I was crowned the first-ever transgender homecoming king of Augsburg! I will never know if I hadn't asked to change the language in voting if I would've been nominated (or even won), but it doesn't matter. The only thing that matters is that I was visible for those who can't be and showed that we are here and belong.

In conclusion, I will never forget the 4 years I spent at Augsburg. They were the highlight of my queer life and pivotal to me becoming the man I am today. I wouldn't be who I am without the love and support of the school administration and the LGBTQIA+ community and family I created and still have today. In my experience, Augsburg was and always will be a place where LGBTQIA+ people are welcomed and celebrated! Augsburg to me will always be synonymous with family and home.

Endnotes

1. In fact, a German journalist named Karl Maria Kertbeny created a foundation of the sexual taxonomy by inventing the words "heterosexual" and "homosexual" in 1868—a year before Augsburg was founded. It took nearly a century for his words to become widely used.

2. Adamo interpreted this image as note passing. Compare his impression to mine, and you can see how the peculiarities of our own perspectives affect our interpretation of the past and the stories we tell about it.

3. "Snoose" is a reference to a type of sniffing tobacco that was popular at the time.

4. Publishing the addresses of people charged with crimes was common for local papers at the time, but we can imagine how it uniquely affected LGBTQIA+ people before legal nondiscrimination protections.

5. Stewart's note: possibly Deb Balzer. See *The Augsburgian*, 1987, page 120.

6. Stewart's note: In *Lawrence v. Texas* (2003) the U.S. Supreme Court ruled that state anti-sodomy laws were unconstitutional. They are still technically on the books in some states but they cannot be enforced.

7. Stewart's note: It was Sverdrup Library at that time, though Lindell undoubtedly still has some of those books.

References

Adamo, P. (2019). *Hold fast to what is good: A history of Augsburg University in 10 objects.* Split Infinitive Books.

Augsburg College Student Personnel Services. (1956). Student Personal History [Form]. Gerda Mortensen Papers. Student Affairs Schedules. "Personal Background" folder. Augsburg University Archives. Minneapolis, MN, United States.

Baker v. Nelson, 291 Minn. 310, 191 N.W.2d 185 (1971).

Bergin, D. P. (2017). *Out north: MNLGBTQ history* [Film]. Twin Cities Public Television, Inc. https://video.tpt.org/video/out–north–mnlgtbq–history–06spot/

Blade, T. T. (1993). Sodom on the Mississippi: The homosexual presence shown in the media. *Hennepin History 2*(2), 4–34. https://digitalcollections.hclib.org/digital/collection/p17208coll13/id/753/rec/1

Danielson, T. (1966, April 4). Night falls: Slum transformed into nocturnal center of metro culture. *The Augsburg Echo*, 3. Augsburg University Archives. Minneapolis, MN, United States. https://archives.augsburg.edu/islandora/object/AUGrepository%3A21788#page/3/mode/2up

Edstrom, J. (1989, March 17). Gay/lesbian paper banned on campus. *The Augsburg Echo*, front page. Augsburg University Archives. Minneapolis, MN, United States. https://archives.augsburg.edu/islandora/object/AUGrepository%3A26049#page/1/mode/2up

Female impersonators fined. (1947, December 1). *The Minneapolis Star*, 17.

Forgotten minorities panel. (1971). [Video file]. Augsburg University Archives. Minneapolis, MN, United States. https://www.youtube.com/watch?v=xlhCK3w8YQg&ab_channel=AugsburgUniversityArchives

Halfhill, R. (1993, November 5). *Oral History of the Minneapolis Gay Liberation Movement* [Interview transcript]. Twin Cities Gay and Lesbian Community Oral History Project, Minnesota Historical Society. Identifier: OH 42.

Jordan, D. (1969, May 18). Campus ministries run a hippie hangout. *The Minneapolis Tribune*, 1B.

Kertbeny, K. M. (1868). [Letter to the editor]. Zeitschrift für Philosophie und philosophische Kritik, *57*(2), 123–139.

Lawrence v. Texas, 539 U.S. 558 (2003).

Mattson, K. (1964, September 30). Work on coffeehouse progresses. *The Augsburg Echo*, 2. Augsburg University Archives. Minneapolis, MN, United States. https://archives.augsburg.edu/islandora/object/AUGrepository%3A21573#page/3/mode/2up

Minneapolis (Minn.) City Planning Commission. (1950). A Plan for the Redevelopment of the Riverside Area. Minneapolis, MN: Commission.[GB1]

Mortensen, G. (1964, June 17). [Letter to L. O. Nyflot]. Gerda Mortensen Papers. Augsburg University Archives. Minneapolis, MN, United States.

Mortensen, G. (1969a, July 29). *Oral History Interview with Gerda Mortensen (1 of 4)* [Interview Transcript]. Augsburg University Archives. Minneapolis, MN, United States. https://archives.augsburg.edu/islandora/object/AUGrepository%3A122288

Mortensen, G. (1969b, July 31). *Oral History Interview with Gerda Mortensen (3 of 4)*. [Interview Transcript]. Augsburg University Archvies. Minneapolis, MN, United States. https://archives.augsburg.edu/islandora/object/AUGrepository%3A122356

Nystuen, N. (1980, October 10). A tradition of 'spontaneous interaction.' *The Augsburg Echo*, 5. Augsburg University Archives. Minneapolis, MN, United States. https://archives. augsburg.edu/islandora/object/AUGrepository%3A24320#page/5/mode/2up

Phelps, K. (1993, November 5). [Interview]. Queer Student Cultural Center Records. Jean-Nickolaus Tretter Collection in GLBT Studies. University of Minnesota.

Schmid, C. F. (1937). *Social saga of two cities: An ecological and statistical study of social trends in Minneapolis and St. Paul*. Monograph Series No. I. Bureau of Social Research, the Minneapolis Council of Social Agencies.

The Augsburgian, 1987 (1987). Augsburg University Archives. Minneapolis, MN, United States. https://archives.augsburg.edu/islandora/object/AUGrepository%3A6565#page/1/ mode/2up

University of Minnesota Libraries. (n.d.). Queer Student Cultural Center Records [Archival material]. Jean-Nickolaus Tretter Collection in GLBT Studies. University of Minnesota.

von Fisher, B. [Conversation with Stewart Van Cleve]. August 2017.

Westergren, E. (2006). *Snoose Boulevard and the golden mile: Swedish immigrant life in Minneapolis in the early 1900s*. Kalmar Läns Museum.

Augsburg's Health Commons:

Caring for Our Neighbors in a World of Extremes

Muna Abdirahman and Kathleen M. Clark

In 1918, Augsburg's graduating class presented the institution with a Silver Loving Cup, the award for an annual oratorical contest. Champions had their names adorned on the cup. The first name on the trophy was in 1922 when future president Bernhard Christensen won with his speech "The Call to Service." A century later, current President Paul Pribbenow leads the university with the conviction that "we are called to serve our neighbor." Service to our neighbor has been a longstanding value and theme of Augsburg University's saga. This deep commitment has fostered educational innovation grounded in location and vocation, mission, and place.

Origins of Service Learning

Much like Bernhard Christiansen, who fervently advanced freedom of intellectual inquiry, his predecessors George Sverdrup and Sven Oftedal resisted the hegemonic establishments of their time. During their professional tenure, both refuted the ivory tower concept of education and believed academic institutions should authentically relate to those they served (Chrislock, 1969, p. 236). Deeply committed to this purpose, Sverdrup required his pre-ministerial students to first gain experience in city congregations. The practice of "Education for Service" has since been a thematic thread woven into the fabric of Augsburg's history.

By 1960, sociology professor and unassuming trailblazer Dr. Joel Torstenson pushed the needle for social change even further. Torstenson was dedicated to transforming the institution's mission of service to a community-led model responsive to and more conscious of its urban settlement. Where others found fault in urban affairs, Torstensen found value. He was a proponent of social justice and place-based civic engagement. His commitment to recognizing the humanity of Augsburg's socially excluded neighbors developed the foundation of the academic program HECUA (Higher Education Consortium for Urban Affairs). It is through programs like this that Augsburg students learn the art of accompaniment.

Education for Service in Action

This commitment to education innovation centered on community-centered experiential learning has allowed Augsburg faculty, staff, and students to respond to the crises of our time in transformative ways. For example, starting in the 1980s, homelessness was visibly on the rise throughout the country. Much of the histories describing the complex set of circumstances that led to these conditions include the gentrification of the urban core, the deinstitutionalization of people with serious and persistent mental illness while federal economic cuts were made to low-income housing programs, structural racism embedded in housing policies, an economic decline including a rise in unemployment for unskilled job markets, and the epidemics of crack cocaine, HIV/AIDS, and the roll-out of the "War on Drugs" (Drier, 2004; Spar, 1984). Minneapolis and the neighborhood to which Augsburg belongs were not spared from these new challenges.

Due to the commitments of Augsburg's leaders to experiential learning and responding to the needs of our neighbors, Professor of Nursing Bev Nillson was able to follow a dream and respond on a human scale to the suffering people were experiencing. Partnering with Central Lutheran Church and the Urban Communities Association of Minneapolis, Nilsson began a Nursing Center (officially named the Augsburg Central Nursing Center [ACNC]) in downtown Minneapolis to provide care to people on the streets. The Fairview Foundation provided $20,000 to launch this effort. Editor Shirley Safgren from *Augsburg Now* (1993) stated, "The Nursing Department is putting Augsburg's motto of 'Education for Service' into direct action by staffing a new Nursing Center that provides much-needed health care to inner city residents" (p. 12). Nilsson stated that the ACNC "gives us the opportunity to practice what we preach. It also allows us, the nursing faculty, to maintain their clinical skills and demonstrate the kind of nursing practice we talk about in the classroom" (Safgren, 1993, p. 12).

Nursing centers during this time were considered to be nurse-led clinics or community centers that offered direct patient care and were often organized by academic institutions (Riesch, 1992). This model of providing care can be traced to the Henry Street Settlement of the late 19th century, the origins of public health nursing (King, 2008). The National League for Nursing's Council of Nursing Centers defined nursing centers as "an organization whose primary mission is to provide nursing services . . . and is owned, operated or controlled by nurses" (1995, p. 1, as cited in Hoffman, 1997). These centers allowed nurses to practice from a more holistic worldview, where care went beyond the constraints of the medical model, and nurses could provide care within the full scope of their licensure. Nursing faculty and students often conducted research and completed required clinical rotations in these spaces. Nursing centers aimed to provide care to those most marginalized to increase access to cost-effective services (Lundeen, 1997).

Janet Labrecque, Nilsson's long-time partner, shared in an oral history (2020) reflecting on the start of the nursing center, "She (Nilsson) was very clear that she wanted it (the ACNC) to be run by nursing . . . she believed strongly in the profession of nursing and that nurses were independent practitioners. . . . this was long before nurse practitioners started . . . She wanted it nursing-centered, community-centered. Feminist theology really was an underpinning to what she wanted to do with students, she felt energized by empowering women to reach their potential personally and professionally" (9:41; 19:24).

The first mission statement of the ACNC was "to prepare registered nurses for professional practice in a changing and expanding discipline by providing clinical educational opportunities for health care that are consistent with Christ's command to care for each other, with the philosophy of the Augsburg College Department of Nursing, and that are carried out among the culturally diverse population in a nurse-managed metropolitan community-based setting" (Augsburg College Center for Nursing, 1994). The ACNC was open on Mondays and Thursdays at the same

time as the free clothing closet (now called " the free store") at Central
Lutheran Church and on Sundays following each of the services. A nurse
coordinator and at least two other nurses (one nursing faculty and one
student) were present each time it was open. Nilsson provided the main
oversight of the ACNC operations, but all the faculty in the Department
of Nursing participated in the activities and care given onsite. Basic supplies and nursing care, such as one-on-one consultations, health referrals,
medication management, and a voucher system, were established for
guests to purchase over-the-counter medications at a nearby pharmacy.
There was no fee for service and names were only recorded in the nursing records for individuals seeking one-on-one nursing care and kept in a
confidential paper chart.

In 1993, the Department of Nursing hosted a nursing theory conference focused on the theory of transcultural nursing (Nelson & Wood,
2000). Nilsson and others presented the ACNC's first-year successes at
the conference. Those in attendance began having conversations about
creating a new nursing program that could integrate the learning experiences at the ACNC into the curriculum for advanced-practice nurses
to care for diverse populations in innovative ways grounded in transcultural nursing theory, giving birth to the Transcultural Community Health
Nursing graduate program (Nelson & Wood, 2000).

As time passed, it became clear that some individuals came to the
ACNC for the relationships that had been established, as guests found
a sense of belonging there. Many guests did not come for any identified
issue but for a place to sit and socialize without having a reason for being
there or interruptions, which is often a rare occurrence for people experiencing homelessness. Soon, rocking chairs were added to the room.
Labrecque shared that Nilsson's favorite memories of the ACNC were
when people would rest in the rocking chairs and share stories as she
soaked their feet. The emphasis on connecting to each other on a human
scale became a central focus of the relationships established at the ACNC.

The Model of Care Unfolds

A decade later, as Professor Nilsson prepared to retire, two new coordinators were hired, Dr. Ruth Enestvedt and Linda Holt. As these faculty members reflected on barriers that guests encountered when entering the

ACNC, the way in which nurses dressed and the equipment they carried was carefully considered. For example, when Nilsson encountered various individuals who opposed her idea of starting the ACNC, she decided nurses would wear white coats and don stethoscopes to convey confidence and professionalism to others. Those doubters also questioned the nurses' abilities to handle any safety concerns that could arise when caring for a room full of unhoused individuals and whether they would know what to do if emergency medical cases presented themselves. Thus, most of the pictures over that first decade included pictures of nurses wearing ironed white coats, donning stethoscopes, and wearing name tags.

Enestvedt, in particular, felt that wearing traditional symbols of professionalized nursing could provide patients with a level of comfort and security in their nurses' skills and expertise. However, for those who have been forced to endure life on the streets, many who have struggled with mental illness, these symbols could also unintendedly instill fear and anxiety. These symbols of professionalism can also be linked to medical research, an original goal of the ACNC. Various accounts have recorded the horrific conditions people, especially people of color, were forced to endure in the name of medical research, such as the infamous Tuskegee experiments and forced sterilizations (Washington, 2006). Endless stories have been shared since the inception of this country on how medical research has caused suffering, pain, and trauma for various individuals and groups, which has led to a deep mistrust for those in healthcare professions, including nurses. Thus, the faculty decided to begin wearing casual clothing and to withhold from carrying medical equipment. A shift in the guest's level of comfort was observed, thus demonstrating that the dress and physical appearance of nurses should align with the cultural norms of the community served and less with professional norms.

Another change that occurred in terms of analyzing possible barriers for guests to enter or engage in the ACNC was the actual physical arrangement of the space. While rocking chairs had been added over time, there was all too often a guest who had been up all night or who required rest. Therefore, Holt and Enestvedt rearranged a small room adjacent to the ACNC to have reclining chairs and blankets, where they could offer someone a safe, quiet place to rest. Other changes were made within the ACNC space to remove any items that may make it seem like a clinic. Enestvedt (2018) described the space before the changes were made:

It was one long room that looked very clinic-y and had dividers and an examination table, it had medicine things, and curtains drawn, and a desk where people had to come to ask for help from the nurses. They had to have a problem to help with. But it was clear that most people were coming for the socks. So we would run from the desk back to behind the curtain and get the socks, back to the curtain, and get socks, and back to the curtain . . . So we moved the socks up front . . . It sort of gradually moved away from you got to come with a problem but what you really want are other things that you need. Let's just start here, instead of starting with, you have to come in here and make up something or ask for something. (36:29)

The faculty wanted the space to feel like a home, a place to belong, connect, and share without proving why someone needed to be there or a time limit on how long one could participate.

Enestvedt also explained that the original idea was that the ACNC would be focused on health promotion, in particular maternal and child health (Enestvedt, 2018). The hope was to actually move it towards more of a clinic model with a provider onsite. In fact, all of the money donated in the first decade was saved in hopes of being able to hire a provider onsite. But as time went on, the center shifted to a more educational focus.

A guest and volunteer who had been at Central before the ACNC started and who continues to be a guest today, Debra Rye, shared her thoughts on this change over time in a 2018 oral history. She stated,

(At the beginning) it was more like you walked in and got some ideas and maybe if there was time you would get your blood pressure taken . . . She (Nilsson) kept records . . . (I would mostly) pick up some hygiene or a pair of socks and go . . . it started out slow . . . (05:13) . . . I kept coming back . . . I developed a rapport with the nurses, and I just kept coming back because they were nice to me. And sometimes we would go out for coffee and talk. They would (Holt and Enestvedt) accompany us to doctor's appointments. And it was the support that I didn't have from other people. (9:35)

When asked about her role as a volunteer she shared, "I know how hard it is to be outside . . . I know how to hold someone's hand who is hungry, because I've been hungry . . . This is a place where I can be here and see people that might be struggling . . . I've just been there with them, because I've been there" (Rye, 2017, 11:06).

In 2012, Holt retired, and Katie Clark was hired to help coordinate the ACNC. Clark was a graduate nursing student in the Masters of Arts in Transcultural Nursing program who had spent time at the ACNC and had previous experiences working with homeless youth in Minneapolis. In the same year, the first cohort of the Doctorate of Nursing Practice began their studies. This degree focused its educational experiences on cultivating students to be transcultural nurse leaders. Enestvedt, one of the faculty members who created this program, which was the first of its kind, had this cohort of nine students create a model of nursing practice for the ACNC along with Clark.

The four-stage model of practice the group created was ahead of its time and was published in various nursing journals. Its purpose was to teach nurses to "decode structures of oppression that exclude individuals from discovering means of health" (Enestvedt et al., 2018, p. 230). The image of the model included a version of a medicine wheel borrowed from the leaders of the Pine Ridge Indian Reservation, individuals who had taught and mentored Augsburg nursing students and faculty over the years. In the center of the wheel is hospitality, which is represented through a Celtic knot, a symbol that "incorporates the design elements of spiral and interlacements portraying the beauty and complexity of human interconnectedness" (Enestvedt et al., 2018, p. 241). Hospitality is the foundation of nursing practice at the ACNC and is a value implicit to the mission of Augsburg. In offering hospitality, students are encouraged to find common ground with guests, connecting on a human scale without an intended agenda.

The first stage of the model of care is acknowledging the need (Enestvedt et al., 2018). This stage is the one in which students begin to acknowledge the level of need of ACNC visitors, and their role is often viewed as a "compassionate caregiver." Students often respond by providing basic necessities such as socks, underwear, and diapers. As guests come to the ACNC, they are not required to have proof of need or to show any identification. No fee for services exists. This often requires nurses to re-think how they engage to create a free, open space that fosters belonging without conditions. Students are encouraged to respond in real time to needs expressed instead of relying on traditional health needs assessments embedded in a deficit thinking model (Enestvedt et al., 2018). Students at this stage also recognized the agency and courage it takes to ask for help. This stage also allows students to explore social injustices and engage in self-reflection as they analyze their biases and become aware of their contributions to structural violence or systemic racism.

In the second stage, nurses are attending to the struggle of those who are marginalized as they move into a role as an "advocate." This is often when guests come and request blood pressure checks or ask a health-related question (Enestvedt et al., 2018). Often, this occurs after the guests are able to establish a sense of trust with the nurses and staff and realize there are no hidden agendas required for seeking care. This is where the nonmedical setting of the nursing center also plays into establishing a safe space. Students are encouraged to practice having conversations, not interviews or assessments. Students are encouraged to avoid questions such as "why," as it can imply judgment and can be a means of controlling the conversation (Enestvedt et al., 2018). Students are also encouraged to participate without intervention, suspending judgment and resisting doing or fixing. During this time students are able to have an opportunity to learn of someone's complex circumstances and learn firsthand how social injustices are experienced. Here, students begin to name structural violence as they authentically listen.

In the third stage, affirming strength, the role of the students becomes a "supporter of agency" of the guest (Enestvedt et al., 2018). This means allowing people agency in naming what they would like for their desired health outcomes and what steps they would like to take regarding the situation at hand. Students focus on naming the strengths they identify in the stories shared with them, which facilitates the relationship moving towards one that is mutually beneficial. Nurses can identify the creative maneuvers that guests use in negotiating the margins and solving problems as they survive life without a permanent residence. Problems should be viewed as "collective" problems, instead of blaming guests for their choices. This also means understanding that these problems are complex, historically grounded, and multifaceted, and are the results of systemic and structural issues such as racism in housing practices (i.e., redlining or racial covenants in property deeds).

In the final stage, accompaniment, the student is in the role of "honoring wisdom." This occurs when a shared wisdom surfaces as the guest and nurses build a relationship embedded in collective agency and problem-solving (Enestvedt et al., 2018). Accompaniment is about walking with someone until the work is "deemed completed by the person or people being accompanied, rather than by the accompagnateur" (Farmer, 2011). This goes beyond the role of an advocate and requires a journey together grounded in epistemological humility, leveled power, and where expertise is de-emphasized. The wisdom the guest has in surviving is viewed as equally important to the nurse's professional training, one not being more important than the other.

As time went on, the ACNC staff needed to respond to new questions and new issues, but always grounded decisions and actions in the model of practice outlined above. The original model of practice also incorporates the stages that a guest experiences as they seek care within the ACNC. This second half of the model has yet to be published or revisited since its inception in 2009. Doing so would require gaining insight and input from our guests, many of whom are not aware of the model we have developed but have voiced the difference in nursing care that they receive at the center.

Growth and Expansion

In 2009, Sahra Noor, a nurse working in the community outreach department at a nearby hospital, reached out to Clark to ask her thoughts on starting another Augsburg College Nursing Center site in the Cedar-Riverside neighborhood, home to Augsburg's campus. Cedar-Riverside is home to over 9,000 individuals, where over 50% of the population is East African, identifying as Somali, Ethiopian, and Oromo (Minnesota Compass, 2022). This four-block area, with multiple high-rise apartment buildings, is mostly public housing units and is said to be the most condensed four-block radius between Chicago and L.A. (Ohikere, 2019). Noor had been part of a participatory action research study in the neighborhood, asking elderly Somali immigrants about their barriers to seeking care in the United States (Pavlish et al., 2010). The women voiced concerns over the lack of faith practices incorporated into care and the lack of culturally competent providers. They felt that issues of worldviews on time and gender also compounded the issues. The Somali women expressed wanting a health-focused drop-in center in the local community that was free of charge and did not require appointments. Again, a lack of trust in health care providers was evident throughout the research findings.

After 2 years of planning and securing space in the densely populated area, a plan was in place. But first, the need for a name change needed to be addressed. As the years went on, most nurse-led clinics became managed by nurse practitioners. While most of these nurse-led clinics (no longer called "nursing centers") continue to stay committed to the original ideals of nursing centers, they have become overall more medically focused clinics. Many of the original nursing centers lacked financial sustainability, especially with the increased costs endured by universities that competed to support such endeavors. Survival depended on third-party reimbursement, which forced many nursing centers to become Federally Qualified Health Centers or merge with established clinics (King, 2008). Therefore, when nursing accreditors came to conduct their site visit at Augsburg, one of the individuals from the accreditation team was confused by the name, "Nursing Center," and why there weren't nurse practitioners completing assessments and providing prescriptions in the space. In addition, leaders at Augsburg and the nearby hospital didn't want people to think the "nursing center" was competing with other organizations who were providing clinic or fee-for-service care. Finally, the way the term "nursing center" translated to the Somali language didn't accurately represent the space. Therefore, the decision was made to change the name of Augsburg Central Nursing Center, as well as the new location in Cedar Riverside, to Health Commons.

In 2011, the Health Commons in Cedar-Riverside (HCCR) was opened through a community-academic partnership consisting of Augsburg University, Fairview Health Systems (a regional care system), the East Africa Health Project (a local nonprofit), and People's Center Clinics and Services (a Federally Qualified Health Center). First located in the women's side of a local mosque, the care was based on the same model of care as the ACNC at Central Lutheran, though the community and needs expressed were quite different. For example, most of the guests have housing, often living in multigenerational public housing units. Instead of seeking basic survival resources, guests are eager to make social connections to one another through health-focused activities such as yoga, swimming, gardening, knitting, and massage. Health education and community forums have also been offered as the guests have asked for help learning about certain issues, such as mental illness or substance use.

The leadership was starkly different at the HCCR location. Instead of one main nurse in charge, there was a team of individuals from various organizations who made daily decisions. The leaders from both the health care system and nonprofit were health care providers who were Somali immigrants. Clark was the only leader who was white and did not speak the language. To ensure the model would be centered on the community's voice, the leadership team hired individuals from the neighborhood to help with language translation and to help recruit individuals to participate in the center's activities. These bilingual community liaisons continue to be the true leaders of the HCCR and have taken on more responsibilities over time.

Enestvedt and Clark co-coordinated the Augsburg Central Health Commons (ACHC) until the mid-2010s when Enestvedt retired. The role of the coordinator has expanded and grown to reach across campus, and now Clark carries the title of executive director of the Augsburg Health Commons. The previous coordinators felt strongly that the Health Commons was a place for only nursing students as they were already licensed nurses, most with years of experience. But, over the years it became clear to Clark that this was a learning opportunity for all Augsburg students. Various undergraduate students have completed internships and required service hours at the Health Commons. The Physician Assistant (PA) program has collaborated with the Department of Nursing, and PA faculty now hold leadership positions within the Health Commons.

Another shift in practice at the Health Commons has been with charting and documentation. For the first two decades, the nurses would spend hours charting their interactions with guests on their health concerns and the discussions or actions taken. Many times guests would provide a different name each time they came in, or they decided not to talk with the nurse once they realized their name would be in a permanent record. Thus, charting changed to be more of a glimpse of who visited. Nurses now provide the same information as 30 years ago, but in the form of check boxes regarding the information. No paper charting occurs. Nurses also either know people's circumstances or don't feel pressure to ask probing questions about their housing situation to record in paper charts. Sometimes nurses don't know if someone is living outside or is housed, but nurses do their best to find out that information or make an educated guess. The priority is not having meticulous charts with data, but focusing on the guest feeling welcomed and allowing them to build trust with the students and nurses.

Responding to a new crisis during the COVID-19 pandemic, the Augsburg Central Health Commons remained open. Clark and Central Lutheran Church staff worked diligently with local health departments, nonprofits, and volunteers to ensure people on the streets had access to basic supplies, food, water, and toileting when buildings were closed. George Floyd had been a guest at Central and the community was deeply impacted by his death. It was a moment in which nurses and volunteers at the ACHC had to show up in new ways to creatively engage and care for guests.

The HCCR was forced to close at the beginning of the COVID-19 pandemic due to lack of space for social distancing. Today, the HCCR is located in two areas within the Riverside Plaza Towers, one mostly used by men and the other by women. During the pandemic, Fairview Health Services applied for a CARES Act Grant to expand HCCR services. This money provided funding to expand to the second space and allowed the HCCR to hire a nurse to be onsite every day of the week. Unfortunately, when the grant funds were exhausted, the financial support to continue having a nurse onsite ended. On Fridays, Augsburg staff, including Physician Assistant students and faculty members, provide foot care services in an elderly public housing unit in the neighborhood.

Funding of the various Health Commons is worth mentioning in this historical analysis of this work, given its longstanding survival in the constantly changing landscape of higher education. The Augsburg Health Commons has depended on donations or small grants since its inception. In the 2010s, a generous donor provided funds to start an endowment for supplies. As the Health Commons has expanded to other locations, these new Health Commons have also relied on grants and donations from the Fairview Foundation. The university supports the work of the Health Commons by employing the faculty who coordinate the Health Commons efforts. Yet, lack of funding overall has always been a challenge, especially regarding sustainable staffing and supply needs.

In 2023, the Health Commons again expanded to two new locations, one in North Minneapolis and the other on the Eastside of St. Paul. These new locations are both partnered with Fairview Health Services and other nonprofits. More faculty from within the nursing department and outside of it are now involved with facilitating this work, which aligns with Nilsson's original idea. A new mission statement was created:

> At the Augsburg Health Commons, we care for individuals, especially those most impacted by racial disparities or the so-called social determinants of health, using innovative approaches that seek to center the voices and dignity of our guests in all we do to accompany one another on a journey of health grounded in solidarity. By engaging in faculty-led learning experiences here, Augsburg students are able to further their understanding of structural inequities, social norms, and care practices that cause harm to individuals and communities. Thus, students are equipped to address the injustices that continue to plague our healthcare systems and have the ability to envision care models that facilitate humanization, utilize co-creation, and can help foster both individual and collective healing. (Augsburg Health Commons, 2023, p. 1)

Other locations are being explored both in Minnesota and beyond.

Lessons from the Past to Forge the Future

Aligned with the mission and values of Augsburg from its inception, leaders of the Health Commons have been the personification of accompaniment. There is a grave misconception in health care that confronting structural inequalities is beyond the scope of the practice. The legacy and professional contributions of the faculty involved with Augsburg Health Commons defy this fallacy. They were instrumental not only in developing the bachelor's and transcultural master's degree nursing programs but also in founding the Health Commons. Unfortunately, Augsburg University is situated in a community that continues to be profoundly impacted by homelessness, and the problem is only getting worse as Minnesota's homeless rate has increased by 10% between 2015 and 2018 (Pittman et al., 2018).

The proliferation of disparities during the pandemic, combined with the aftermath of George Floyd's murder, was a traumatic time for the city of Minneapolis. The world experienced the ripple effect of pain as they watched the city burn down on the news. The need to address health inequity and systemic racism became increasingly evident. During these unprecedented times, we realized that the health of all of us depended on the health of each of us. It is even more incumbent upon us to practice radical hospitality in such times as these. Hospitality extends beyond tolerance or welcoming; it creates space so a stranger can enter and become a friend instead of an enemy (Nouwen, 1975).

It is through the innovative transcultural nursing model used at the Augsburg Health Commons that over 1,600 students learn to serve diverse individuals in an atmosphere of mutuality. Over 75,000 visitors have received critical services from preventative care, warm meals, necessary personal hygiene products, and care packages. Through this innovative approach to care through relationship and connection, students, too, are changed. By recognizing injustice and examining why it exists, students must come to a holistic understanding of individuals and society. The Health Commons model of care allows nurses and students to practice a base-up approach that fosters peace, harmony, and just conditions for health and well-being. It creates a call for action and mobilizes students to challenge the way things are. But a call to action begins first through relationships built on trust that allow space for people to unpack their fears and concerns. After all, relationships are primary; all else is derivative.

References

Augsburg College Center for Nursing. (1994). *Mission Statement* [Unpublished Annual Report]. Augsburg University.

Augsburg Health Commons (2023). *Augsburg Health Commons: Vision Statement, Mission Statement, + Goals for 2023–2024* [Unpublished Document]. Augsburg University.

Chrislock, C. (1969). *From fjord to freeway: 100 years, Augsburg College*. Augsburg College.

Drier, P. (2004, May 1). Reagan's legacy: Homelessness in America. *Shelterforce.org*. https://shelterforce.org/2004/05/01/reagans-legacy-homelessness-in-america/

Enestvedt, R. (2018, February 20). *Interview by Kathleen Clark*. [Digital Recording]. Oral Histories—Health Commons. Augsburg University Archives. Minneapolis, MN, United States. https://archives.augsburg.edu/islandora/object/AUGrepository%3AOralHistoriesHealthCommonsEnestvedt2018

Enestvedt, R.C., Clark, K.M., Freborg, K., Miller, J.P., Leuning, C.J., Schuhmacher, D., McHale, K., Baumgartner, K., & Loushin, S. (2018). Caring in the margins: A scholarship of accompaniment for advanced transcultural nursing practice. *Advances in Nursing Science, 41*(3), 230–242. doi: 10.1097/ANS.0000000000000201

Farmer, P. (2011). *Accompaniment as policy* [Transcript of a commencement address at the Harvard Kennedy School of Government]. Office of the Secretary-General's Special

Adviser on Community-Based Medicine & Lessons from Haiti. https://www.lessons fromhaiti.org/press-and-media/transcripts/accompaniment-as-policy/

Hoffman, S. E. (1997). Professional practice: Nursing centers – models of professional practice. *Journal of Professional Nursing, 13*(6), 335.

King, E. S. (2008). A 10-year review of four academic nurse-managed centers: Challenges and survival strategies. *Journal of Professional Nursing, 24*(1), 14–20.

Labrecque, J. (2020, March 7). *Interview by Kathleen Clark.* [Digital Recording]. Nursing Department Oral Histories. Augsburg University Archives. Minneapolis, MN, United States. https://archives.augsburg.edu/islandora/object/AUGrepository%3AOral HistoriesLabrecque2020.

Lundeen, S. P. (1997). Community nursing centers—issues for managed care. *Nursing Management, 28*(3), 35–37.

Minnesota Compass. (2022). *Cedar Riverside neighborhood data* [Data set]. Minnesota Compass. https://www.mncompass.org/profiles/city/minneapolis/cedar–riverside

Nelson, R. C., & Wood, D. (2000). *The Anderson chronicles: An intimate portrait of Augsburg College 1963–1997.* Kirk House Publishers.

Nouwen, H. (1975). *Reaching out: The three movements of the spiritual life.* Doubleday.

Ohikere, O. (2019, Oct 24). Little Mogadishu on the Mississippi: Minnesota's Somali Americans strive to free their community from violence. *World.* https://wng.org/articles/ little-mogadishu-on-the-mississippi-1617298219

Pavlish, C.L., Noor, S., & Brandt, J. (2010). Somali immigrant women and the American health care system: Discordant beliefs, divergent expectations, and silent worries. *Social Science and Medicine, 71,* 353–361.

Pittman, B., Nelson-Dusek, S., Gerrard, M.D., & Shelton, E. (2018). *Homelessness in Minnesota: Detailed findings from the 2018 Minnesota homeless study.* Amherst H. Wilder Foundation. https://www.wilder.org/wilder-research/research-library/homelessness-minnesota-detailed-findings-2018-minnesota-homeless

Riesch, S. K. (1992). Nursing centers. *Annual Review of Nursing Research, 10*(1), 145. DOI: 10.1891/0739–6686.10.1.145

Rye, D. (2017, November 17). *Interview by Kathleen Clark.* [Digital Recording]. Oral Histories—Health Commons. Augsburg University Archives. Minneapolis, MN, United States. https://archives.augsburg.edu/islandora/object/AUGrepository%3AOral HistoriesHealthCommonsDebraRye2017

Safgren, S. (1993, March). Education for service in action...Nursing department staffs new inner city nursing center. *Augsburg Now,* 12. Augsburg University Archives. Minneapolis, MN, United States. https://archives.augsburg.edu/islandora/object/AUG repository%3A35259#page/13/mode/2up

Spar, K. (1984, September 14). *The homeless: Overview of the problem and the federal response.* Congressional Research Service Library of Congress. https://www.every crsreport.com/files/19840914_84–766EPW_751216af033416b98d5fdde6999891b8f1f c5c2c.pdf

Washington, H. A. (2006). *Medical apartheid: The dark history of medical experimentation on Black Americans from colonial times to the present.* Doubleday Publishing.

Holding the Door Open:

• •

Access, Alternatives, and Agitation —Who Will Be the Next "First"?

Terrance Kwame-Ross

> *"When you see people call themselves revolutionary, always talking about destroying, destroying, destroying but never talking about building or creating, they're not revolutionary. They do not understand the first thing about revolution. It's creating."*
>
> —Kwame Ture

Revisiting, Rethinking, and Reclaiming Revolutionary and Radical Roots

At Augsburg, we hold the door open for each other—literally and figuratively! When crossing campus, we wait at the door so that others may join us, and in the world we hold the door open for those who are "first" to join us from their particular places, experiences, and identities. It's fundamental to the history of this institution and to our calling as a university of "firsts."

As we explore "firsts" at Augsburg University, we start at the very beginning of its roots, recalling Martin Luther nailing his Ninety-Five Theses to the door of the Castle Church, in Wittenberg, Germany in 1517, sparking the Protestant Reformation that eventually led to a divorce and the split of the Western Church—a religious revolution: a powerful act of creating, and an opening!

Luther's actions pointed to a new route, a return to that which is "true and good," though this revolution was not without acrimony and conflict. It seems that revolution for creation requires vision, planning, responsibility, sacrifice, and neighborly love. Revolution, and the power to create and be creative, is part of Augsburg's historical DNA. Our beginning, a type of "first," helped set in motion a dynamic history for Augsburg that gave birth to the first seminary founded by Norwegian Lutherans in America, that morphed into Augsburg Theological Seminary, then Augsburg College and Theological Seminary, then Augsburg College, and now Augsburg University! There is a long history of "firsts" here.

Throughout its history, Augsburg has managed to "hold the door open" in order to stay true to the commitment to provide access to a quality education for all. Augsburg emerged in 1869 in the aftermath of the Civil War, and then lived on through Reconstruction, World War I, the Great Depression, World War II, the Civil Rights Movement, COVID-19, the economic and racial reckoning in 2020—specifically the murder of George Floyd by Minneapolis Police—and we are still here! And we remain a vibrant racial, ethnic, linguistic, socioeconomic, religious, sexual orientation, gender, and dis/abilities diverse learning environment.

There are myriad examples of how Augsburg has flourished throughout its history, but there also are moments when Augsburg's door was closed. For example, it was 1921 before women were admitted to Augsburg and even longer before nonwhite students found a home at the university.

Augsburg has a history and memory to tap into for reconciliation, recovery, and rediscovery of the power and meaning of "firsts." Given the fact that Augsburg was first established as an all-white, male, heterosexual, Christian institution (cis male), the integration of females, followed by other immigrants, and then a variety of cultural, religious, racial, ethnic, linguistic, and sexual and gender differing populations, all makes for an interesting and powerful history. Our history of "firsts" can stimulate and provoke bonds within and outside of the university, where everyone knows, but might not be able to name the "air about this place." How does Augsburg exist with so much access, alternatives, and possible agitation? How are "firsts" even accomplished in this place? The answers to these questions are found in our identity: Augsburg's saga.

What Is Augsburg's Saga and How Does It Relate to "First?"

As President Paul Pribbenow has written (2014),

Augsburg University's saga runs deep in the culture and meaning of our work together. An exploration of Augsburg's history surfaces several themes that are central to our saga: an immigrant sensibility shaped in an urban neighborhood, freedom through faith to ask tough questions and engage otherness, a moral commitment to access to quality education for all, and the vocational aspiration to be neighbor to and with each other. (p. 150)

Together these themes inform Augsburg's identity and its abiding commitment to faithfulness and generosity in its place.

Like all good stories, Augsburg's history is grounded in everyday life events and the mundane world—individuals and groups at work, in family, at school, at church, in neighborhoods, and building community. Augsburg has stories of "first" that are grounded in real people's lives, in place, environment, time, and the push and pull of institutional and societal histories and pressures. We are attempting to have conversations with social, individual, and institutional history, and conversations with each other with our biographies, all of which is part of a social process. Social processes can limit or expand opportunity, freedom, justice, neighborly love, and access—all ways of being "first." For Augsburg, we can point to a powerful list of "firsts":[1]

- A first public disputation against the Catholic Church when Luther nailed Ninety-Five Theses to the Castle Church in Wittenberg, Germany in 1517

- First Seminary founded by Norwegian Lutherans in America, Marshall, WI: Augsburg Seminary, 1869

- First President of Augsburg: August Weenas, 1869

- First Move/Relocation: Marshall, WI to Minneapolis, 1872

- First name change: Augsburg Seminary to Augsburg College and Theological Seminary, 1917

- First year that women were admitted as students: 1921

- First woman in a formal leadership position at Augsburg: Gerda Mortenson, Dean of Women, 1923

- First Latinx woman to serve as faculty at Augsburg: Mimi Kingsley (born in Mexico), 1948.

- First Asian American Pacific Islander woman to serve as faculty: Khin Khin Jensen (born in Burma/Myanmar), 1959.

- First Black women hired as faculty at Augsburg: Mary T. Howard, 1965–1967; Vivian Jenkins Nelsen, the first to teach at Augsburg full time, 1969.

- First director of Pan-Afrikan Center (formerly Office of Black Student Affairs): Betsye Addison, circa 1970 (also served as a communications instructor), soon followed by her husband, Terry Addison in 1972, perhaps the first Black man to work full time at Augsburg

- First director of "American Indian Program": Bonnie Wallace, 1978

- First full-time director of "Latino Student Services": Eloisa Echávez, 1993

- First non-Norwegian president: William Frame, 1997

- First alumnus Nobel Prize Winner: Peter Agre, 2003

- First director of "GLBTQA Student Services": Jay Weisner, 2004

Given this list, what is the meaning of "first," at Augsburg? My research in the Augsburg archives points to four dimensions of "first" in Augsburg's saga. These relate to, and overlap with, individual and institutional narratives.

To begin, "first" is positional. Think order, hierarchy, and sequence. Augsburg hires, accepts, and places people into "first." For example, Dr. Richard Green became the first Black administrative leader in the 1980s, serving as Vice President of Academic Affairs and Dean of College. Vice President Green's breakthrough, and Augsburg's open door, made possible the diversification of the institution's positions and roles.

Second, "first" denotes direction, a way, a path, an orientation. There are many decisions that had to be made about the "direction" of Augsburg throughout its history. Some have been written about and explored in the previous chapters. The move from Wisconsin to Minnesota, the separation of the preparatory school from the college, and then the seminary from the university; becoming coeducational; and more recently, a direct admissions approach that increases access to higher education. These all point to a direction, for the institution, and who it serves.

Third, "firsts" emerge from vocation. Augsburg has a vocation—to "educate students to be informed citizens, thoughtful stewards, critical thinkers, and responsible leaders." Augsburg's reliance on its mission and deep commitment to values of service and stewardship is lived out as it educates individuals to reflect these values in their own vocations in society. This leads to our students living out the vocation of being "first" in all kinds of ways in the world!

Finally, "first" is personal. Individuals, often representatives of a group, have accomplishments. Because the university is made up of people, there will be "first" generation student acceptance, success, and graduation from college. Faculty and staff will be the "firsts" to be hired into higher education, and then promoted and tenured. And within the staff, there will be individual "firsts" to celebrate.

My own narrative integrates all four definitions and dimensions of "first" here at Augsburg, and elsewhere. I am an African American male, descendant of enslaved Africans in the United States. I work as a tenured professor of education, where I teach critical histories and philosophies of education, school and society, social studies methods, and learning and development courses in the Elementary Teacher Education Program. My racial, cultural, and linguistic background situates and invites me to be "first" here at Augsburg, in my position, in the field of education, and in my family, neighborhood, and community. For me and Augsburg, "first" is tied up and aligns itself with social justice relating to diversity and equity of race, gender, sexual orientation, religion, and ethnicity.

Inevitably, "firsts" help us challenge traditional and cultural ways of thinking, particularly as we consider who has access to certain social worlds, roles, and opportunities within Augsburg and across broader society. Augsburg must contend with the larger social forces of racism, white supremacy, anti-Semitism, anti-Muslim sentiment, hate crimes, and the exclusion of culturally and racial diverse groups from political and economic justice. We can see throughout Augsburg's history that by "holding the door open" to people with a wide range of backgrounds and experiences, this institution has led the way in breaking through social restrictions and injustices. These can be identified in Augsburg's achievements, individually and collectively, as powerful, purposeful, and meaningful "firsts."

The next "firsts" at Augsburg

Universally across all human histories and groups, people have immigrated, migrated, protested, fought, and died for personal and collective freedom, including relief from land invasion and political, cultural, religious, racial, ethnic, gender, linguistic, and sexual persecution. Augsburg's historical saga is part of this larger social narrative, and so are all of our individual and ancestral stories. Human beings want to live, work, play, and love in peace, safety, and freedom. This pushing through "doors" and "opening doors" will inevitably produce "firsts." After all, Augsburg has its roots in revolutionary action that is riddled with dispute, protest, dissension, and reform against error, abuse, and totalizing power in order to find a path "through truth to freedom."

What a saga! From a meager beginning, Augsburg has overcome and triumphed through creative hard work, relying on the will to survive, the power to change, and the courage to cut ties and start over again. This history reflects the character of all the "firsts" who have come through Augsburg over our many years. We have a capacity for work, use of mind, spirit, and heart, in service to family, church, neighborhood, community, and society. Some of us are, and will be, "first," here at Augsburg, and will go out into the world and make history to be "first" again. Here, you can make and tell your own stories. Here too, we can search our own historical archives and recover stories that have been lost and found, and tell them in the hope that they will create a stronger bond between us and all others. The *Minneapolis Spoken Recorder*, on February 17, 1950, featured the headline: "Need Not Search For Brotherhood, Christensen says." The story includes a quote from Augsburg's sixth president, Bernhard Christensen:

> We need not search for Brotherhood in vain to the ends of the earth. Like Ali Hafed's acres of diamonds, it is here at our feet, in our own city, in our own churches, **at our very doors**.

Indeed, it is at Augsburg's very door. When it is opened, the next "first" has happened, is happening, and will happen. This is so because we make history, we are and become "firsts." Our calling and challenge is to think beyond now, and to plan, to be visionary, even revolutionary, to hold the door open for the next "firsts" at Augsburg. I leave you with: *Who are the next "firsts"? Will it be you?!*

Endnote

1.   Readers are encouraged to explore the Augsburg University Archives, including written and oral history collections, for fascinating documentation and interviews about many of these "firsts." Visit archives.augsburg. edu.

References

Need not search for brotherhood, Christiansen says (1950, February 17). *Minneapolis Spokesman Recorder*. https://newspapers.mnhs.org/jsp/PsImageViewer.jsp?doc_id=6ff34a0f-54f7-4bc3-861a-d07acb7dba65%2Fmnhi0031%2F1DFIOV5F%2F50021701

Pribbenow, P. (2014). Lessons on vocation and location: The saga of Augsburg College as urban settlement. *Word & World, 34*(2), 149–159.

Authors and Participants

• •

in The Saga Project

Muna Abdirahman, DNP, '22,
Graduate of the Doctor in Nursing Practice program

Katie Bishop, J.D.,
Special Assistant to the President and former Vice President for Student
Success and Experience

Berlynn Bitengo, '21,
Former President of the Augsburg Student Government

Eric Buffalohead, Ph.D.,
Associate Professor and Chair of the American Indian, Indigenous, and
First Nations Studies Department

Babette Chatman, '06,
University Pastor and Director of Campus Ministries

Kathleen M. Clark, DNP,
Associate Professor, Chair of the Nursing Department, and Executive
Director of the Augsburg Health Commons

William Green, Ph.D.,
Professor Emeritus of History

Jenny Hanson, Ph.D., '05,
Associate Professor of Film, Communication Studies, and New Media

Terrance Kwame-Ross, Ph.D.,
Martin Olav Sabo Endowed Chair in Public Service and Citizenship
and Associate Professor of Education

Paul Pribbenow, Ph.D.,
President of the University

Stewart Van Cleve, M.U.S., M.L.I.S.,
Director of the Library and University Archivist

Knaunong "Birdy" Xiong, '23

Index

. . . .